The Ideology Contagion

How Ideas Go Viral

by
Peter Whitmore

Peter Whitmore

"A revolution is an idea, taken up by bayonets."

— *Napoleon Bonaparte*

Peter Whitmore

Table of Contents

Introduction

Ideas shape our world. They influence our decisions, mold our societies, and drive the course of history. But how do some ideas spread like wildfire while others fizzle out? In "The Ideology Contagion: How Ideas Go Viral," we explore the fascinating mechanisms behind the rapid dissemination of ideologies in our interconnected world.

Picture yourself scrolling through social media, encountering a meme that perfectly captures a complex political situation. Within hours, it's shared by millions, sparking debates and shaping opinions. Or consider how a hashtag can mobilize global movements, transcending borders and cultures. These are just glimpses of the power of ideological contagion.

This book takes you on a journey through the psychological, social, and technological factors that fuel the viral nature of ideas. We'll examine how our minds are wired to latch onto certain concepts, how social networks amplify messages, and how technology has revolutionized the speed and reach of information sharing.

From political revolutions to internet phenomena, we'll dissect real-world case studies that illustrate the far-reaching impacts of viral ideologies. You'll gain insights into why some ideas catch on while others don't, and how this knowledge can be applied in various fields, from marketing to social activism.

As we navigate this exploration together, you'll develop a critical lens for evaluating the ideas you encounter daily. By understanding the mechanics of ideological contagion, you'll be better equipped to engage with information responsibly and contribute meaningfully to the conversations shaping our world.

Prepare to dive into a fascinating exploration of how ideas spread, evolve, and change the world around us.

Peter Whitmore

Chapter 1: The Viral Nature of Ideas

Unveiling the Virus Metaphor

Imagine this: you're walking down a busy street, your phone buzzing with notifications, and among the chatter of voices, you hear a catchy song drifting through the air. It's the latest viral hit, and before you know it, you're humming along, maybe even sharing it with your friends. You didn't go out looking for it, yet here you are, joining a huge crowd of people who have fallen for this infectious tune. This scene isn't just about music; it's a metaphor for how ideas spread through society—just like a virus.

When we talk about ideas being "viral," we're tapping into a powerful metaphor that really connects with our everyday lives. This comparison means a lot more than just clever wording; it encourages us to think about how ideas spread, grow, and sometimes even change, much like biological viruses do. Just as a virus needs a host to thrive, ideas need people and communities to come alive and spread.

Let's start by defining what we mean by 'viral ideas.' A viral idea is one that grabs people's attention or interest, making them want to share it with others. This sharing can happen through conversations, social media, books, or even casual chats. Think about it: how many times have you come across a concept or belief that resonated so much with you that you just had to pass it along? Maybe it was a thought-provoking article that sparked a lively debate among friends or a funny meme that made you laugh and prompted you to send it to a group chat. These moments capture the heart of viral ideas—they catch on, encouraging others to share and spread them.

Now that we've got a handle on what viral ideas are, let's dig deeper into the traits of viruses and how they relate to the spreading of ideas. Viruses are fascinating; they have unique skills that help them infect hosts effectively. For example, they can replicate themselves quickly and adapt to their surroundings. Similarly, ideas can change and evolve, often becoming more interesting or relevant as they move through different settings. A simple thought can develop into a complex belief system, gaining depth as it interacts with various cultures and personal experiences.

Let's talk about something called "viral load." In the world of infectious diseases, viral load refers to how much virus is in an infected person, which relates to how easily it can spread to others. Applying this idea to concepts, we can think of viral load as the appeal or power of a particular idea. Some concepts are naturally more persuasive, tapping into values or beliefs that resonate strongly with specific groups or the general public. When an idea has a high viral load, it's more likely to be embraced and shared, creating a ripple effect that can lead to significant societal change.

Another key part of viruses is their vectors—the ways in which they spread from one person to another. When we think about how ideas move, we can identify several channels, such as face-to-face conversations, books, digital platforms, and social media. Each of these channels serves as a way to carry ideas from one person to another, helping them reach a wider audience. For example, social media sites like Twitter or TikTok have become popular channels for viral ideas, allowing for fast sharing and interaction across the globe.

Let's pause for a moment to consider something we all know well: memes. These simple, often funny images or phrases have become a big part of our culture, spreading like wildfire online. Memes serve both as carriers and channels for ideas, packing complex emotions into easy-to-understand formats. They often rely on shared cultural references, tapping into common experiences that encourage people to share them widely. The speed and simplicity of creating and sharing memes highlight the viral nature of ideas, showing just how quickly they can embed themselves in our minds and become part of everyday talk.

To further illustrate this idea, think about the incredible success of the Ice Bucket Challenge. What started as a grassroots campaign to raise awareness for Amyotrophic Lateral Sclerosis (ALS) quickly turned into a worldwide movement, engaging millions of people in just a few weeks. The challenge itself was straightforward: dump a bucket of ice water on your head, challenge others to do the same, and donate to ALS research. The mix of a fun idea, the surprise factor, and the power of social media created the perfect environment for this concept to spread virally. It showed how an infectious idea can have real effects, getting people involved in a cause and raising significant funds for research.

Now that we've laid out the main pieces of our virus metaphor, it's important to recognize how these elements interact with one another. Just like a virus may thrive in certain settings while struggling in others, ideas also face different levels of acceptance based on the social and cultural backdrop they come from. Some ideas might find a warm welcome in specific communities, attracting passionate supporters, while others might not catch on and are simply overlooked or dismissed.

Understanding how viral ideas spread gives us the tools to evaluate their impact. When we examine how infectious ideas replicate, adapt, and find their audiences, we start to see the complex web of influence that shapes our beliefs, actions, and culture. We are not just passive recipients of ideas; we actively participate in this viral environment, deciding which concepts we want to accept, challenge, and share.

As we navigate this landscape, our personal stories can serve as vivid examples of our interactions with viral ideas. Think back to the last time you had a heated discussion about a trending topic or shared a news article that got everyone talking. How did these ideas take root in your mind? What made you decide to share them? Perhaps you were struck by the emotions they stirred, or maybe they mirrored your beliefs in a way that felt important.

By reflecting on our own experiences with viral ideas, we can gain a better understanding of how they infiltrate our lives. This exploration is much like tracing the spread of a virus; it involves examining the paths through which ideas travel and the people they affect. We become more aware of the influences that shape our thoughts and actions, creating an atmosphere that encourages thoughtful reflection and engagement.

As we continue this exploration of the viral nature of ideas, we are ready to look at how these concepts have appeared throughout history. From revolutionary movements to shifts in culture, the influence of viral ideas has dramatically shaped societies and deeply affected individuals' lives. Understanding how these ideas work not only helps us grasp the past but also prepares us to engage thoughtfully with the beliefs and ideologies shaping our present and future.

The metaphor of viral ideas offers us a way to examine our world—one that emphasizes the need to be careful hosts. As we navigate a landscape filled with ideas competing for our attention, knowing how they spread helps us make better choices about which ones to embrace and share. The next time you find yourself sending a video, stirring up a debate, or simply thinking about a new concept, take a moment to consider the viral nature of that experience. What made it resonate with you? How might it influence the thoughts and actions of others?

The relationship between ideas and society is intricate and ever-changing, and as we peel back the layers of this metaphor, we start to reveal the power of the stories we choose to carry forward. Our journey into understanding the viral nature of ideas is just beginning, and with it comes the chance to engage more meaningfully with the beliefs that shape our lives and the world around us.

Historical Instances of Ideological Outbreaks

Throughout human history, there have been pivotal moments when powerful ideas burst forth, reshaping societies and altering cultures in significant ways. These ideological outbreaks, much like a viral wave, can swiftly sweep through communities and nations, touching hearts and minds with incredible speed. Each instance reveals how viewpoints can change, beliefs can adapt, and movements can spring to life, driven by the cultural climate, the emotional pull of ideas, and often, advancements in technology. By looking at key moments in history, we can better understand how ideas take root and thrive, ultimately breaking down old ways of thinking.

Consider the Protestant Reformation, a major turning point in the history of Christianity. In the early 16th century, a monk named Martin Luther sparked a movement that would change the religious landscape forever. What ignited this change? Luther's 95 Theses—a list of complaints against the Catholic Church—that he famously nailed to the door of the Wittenberg Castle Church. But these ideas weren't just confined to the church walls or heard by a select few; they spread rapidly, largely due to the invention of the printing press.

The printing press, created by Johannes Gutenberg in the mid-15th century, was much more than just a piece of technology; it was a groundbreaking tool that amplified the spread of ideas. It allowed for the quick reproduction of texts, making literature, pamphlets, and religious writings accessible to more people than ever before. In a time when many were still illiterate, the printed word became a powerful means to share thoughts and beliefs. Luther's 95 Theses found their way into the hands of the literate middle class, resonating deeply with those who felt neglected by the Church's practices, such as the sale of indulgences, which Luther strongly opposed.

The emotional appeal of Luther's message was profound. His arguments struck a chord with people who were growing increasingly frustrated with the authority of institutions. The Reformation gave a voice to those seeking a more personal connection to their faith, emphasizing that individuals could interpret scriptures for themselves. This idea was groundbreaking; it suggested that people could have a direct relationship with God, bypassing the clergy. As this notion gained traction, it transformed the socio-political landscape. New religious movements emerged, challenging not only the Church but the political norms of the time.

Luther's ideas ignited passion across Europe, leading to the formation of various Protestant denominations. The Reformation didn't just splinter Christianity; it set the stage for wider societal changes. Questioning religious authority began to influence other areas of life, leading into the Enlightenment—a period marked by reason, individualism, and skepticism of traditional power. What started as a theological argument became a driving force for significant shifts in governance, education, and the pursuit of knowledge.

Fast forward a few centuries, and we encounter another significant ideological outbreak: the Enlightenment. This intellectual movement flourished in the 17th and 18th centuries, driven by a thirst for knowledge, reason, and scientific exploration. Philosophers like Voltaire, Rousseau, and Locke promoted ideas that helped topple tyrannies and oppressive governments. The Enlightenment wasn't limited to one region; it spread through salons and pamphlets, capturing the imaginations of countless individuals across Europe and beyond.

What made the Enlightenment stand out was its ability to link diverse ideas and foster conversations among thinkers from different fields. The power of the printing press once again proved invaluable, enabling the swift spread of revolutionary thoughts. The written word became a tool for challenging established norms and proposing new ideas for governance and society. The effects were monumental, leading to revolutions such as the American and French Revolutions, which echoed the ideals of liberty, equality, and fraternity promoted by Enlightenment thinkers.

The Enlightenment's focus on reason and individual rights laid the groundwork for concepts like democracy and human rights. The ripple effects of these ideas reached around the globe, inspiring movements for social justice and reform. This demonstrates how ideological outbreaks can trigger major changes in societal structures, often with consequences that extend far beyond their initial origins.

As we move into more recent times, the ways in which ideas spread have changed, but the basic principles remain the same. The Arab Spring, for instance, is a modern example that showcases how technology can enhance the spread of ideas and spur movements for change. Beginning in 2010, a wave of protests and uprisings swept across the Arab world, challenging long-standing autocratic regimes. Social media platforms, particularly Facebook and Twitter, became vital tools for organizing protests, sharing information, and rallying supporters.

The power of the Arab Spring lay not just in the dire situations faced by many citizens but also in the strength of collective action. Activists utilized social media to share stories of resistance, highlighting the injustices their communities faced. This created a sense of unity that crossed borders, as images and narratives from Tunisia inspired protests in Egypt, Libya, Syria, and beyond. The speed of social media allowed local issues to become part of a global conversation about democracy, human rights, and freedom.

However, the Arab Spring also highlights the complexities that come with ideological outbreaks. While the initial protests led to significant political changes in some areas, the results have been mixed. In certain instances, governments adapted their strategies to suppress dissent, while in other cases, the chaos gave way to civil conflict. These outcomes remind us of the unpredictable nature of how ideas spread and the various factors that influence their success.

Another notable contemporary movement is Black Lives Matter, which arose in response to systemic racism and police violence in the United States. Following the tragic deaths of individuals like Trayvon Martin, Michael Brown, and George Floyd, the movement gained traction through grassroots organizing and the power of social media. Hashtags like #BlackLivesMatter flooded online platforms, drawing attention to issues of racial injustice and inequality.

The success of this movement in spreading its message can be attributed to the unique combination of emotional resonance and the facilitation of technology. The strong reactions to injustice, alongside the immediacy of digital communication, united communities worldwide. Protests erupted not only in American cities but also in nations far removed from the initial incidents, showcasing the strength of shared ideas in our interconnected world. Images and videos of the protests spread rapidly, sparking conversations about race relations, systemic inequality, and the need for social reform.

The Black Lives Matter movement serves as a clear example of how ideological outbreaks remain relevant today. It shows that the spread of ideas is not just an academic concept; it has real consequences that can lead to policy changes, shifts in cultural attitudes, and renewed discussions about justice and equality.

Looking back at these historical examples of ideological outbreaks helps us recognize that the spread of ideas is not just a passive event but a dynamic force that profoundly shapes societies. The Reformation, the Enlightenment, the Arab Spring, and movements like Black Lives Matter reveal a complex web of connections among psychological influences, cultural contexts, and technological advances. These outbreaks demonstrate how ideas can inspire action, challenge the status quo, and reshape our world.

As we navigate the challenges of our modern landscape—filled with competing ideas and rapid shifts—understanding historical instances of ideological outbreaks can offer valuable lessons. We must examine the interplay of ideas, technology, and social dynamics critically, as each moment of ideological contagion provides insights into our shared journey. Ultimately, these examples remind us of the strength of ideas, showing that they can serve as either a means of liberation or a spark for conflict, depending on the context in which they arise. The real challenge lies in deciding which ideas we choose to support and share, as they hold the power to shape our future in ways we may not fully grasp yet.

The Speed of Modern Virality

In a world where we constantly scroll through our smartphones, the way ideas spread has become incredibly fast-paced. Not too long ago, sharing an idea was like a slow train winding its way through the countryside. Now, thanks to technology, that journey resembles a high-speed bullet train that blasts through barriers, completely changing how we communicate. The digital age has created a whirlwind of thought and expression, with social media acting as the main highway for sharing ideas, beliefs, and movements.

The way we think about virality has changed along with technology. In the past, ideas spread slowly, through chance encounters or hand-written pamphlets. Now, with just one click, an idea can reach millions. Social media algorithms play a huge role in this, acting as both gatekeepers and megaphones that decide which ideas get noticed and which fade away into the background. This new environment calls for a closer look at how things work behind the scenes and what psychological factors make certain ideas catch on faster than others.

One of the most noticeable aspects of digital platforms is the creation of echo chambers—places where people are surrounded by views that mirror their own. In these spaces, ideas can take off like a spark igniting dry grass, as users engage with content that resonates with them while ignoring opposing viewpoints. This isn't just a quirk of human behavior; it's built into the very fabric of social media. Algorithms prioritize engagement, so posts that stir up strong emotions—whether it's joy, anger, or sadness—are the ones that get shared the most. This creates a cycle that can fuel extreme opinions and deepen divisions.

Think about influencers—people who have the ability to sway opinions and set trends online. They are like the celebrities of the digital age, with a reach that goes far beyond traditional media. Influencers carefully craft their images, balancing authenticity with strategic promotion of ideas and products. The strong emotional connection they build with their followers is what makes them so effective. When an influencer supports an idea or movement, it can spread like wildfire because their followers are not just passive watchers; they actively help share the message.

Take the Ice Bucket Challenge from 2014 as a perfect example. It started as a fun way to raise awareness for ALS (Amyotrophic Lateral Sclerosis) by having people pour cold water over themselves. What began as a simple challenge turned into a global sensation. Celebrities, politicians, and everyday folks joined in, sharing videos that showed not just their support for the cause, but also their willingness to have a good time. The mix of entertainment, emotional connection, and community spirit created a powerful force, raising millions for ALS research and significantly increasing awareness about the disease.

Several psychological factors contribute to why some ideas go viral. First and foremost, emotional impact matters; ideas that make people feel strongly—whether through anger, happiness, or empathy—are more likely to grab attention and get shared. Relatability also plays a big part; ideas that people can see themselves in tend to catch on more easily. The desire for social acceptance adds another layer, as individuals often gravitate towards ideas that will earn them approval from their peers, which can lead to a kind of groupthink that silences dissenting opinions.

However, the fast pace at which ideas spread isn't without its downsides. The digital world often becomes a hotbed for misinformation, where false claims can thrive right alongside accurate information. Once an idea—true or false—takes off online, it can be very hard to rein it in. Misinformation can spread faster than the truth, as we saw during the COVID-19 pandemic. From the start, a flood of false narratives and conspiracy theories circulated online, complicating public health efforts and causing widespread fear and confusion.

Polarization is another worrying outcome of how quickly ideas can spread. In echo chambers, more moderate voices can be drowned out, creating a split society where compromise becomes nearly impossible. This situation has serious implications. As communities become more divided, the chance for conflict increases, and productive conversations often turn into hostility and mistrust.

It's essential to recognize the role of movements that have harnessed social media for change when discussing the virality of ideas today. The #MeToo movement is a standout example, emerging as a powerful response to the pervasive issues of sexual harassment and assault. What started as a simple hashtag grew into a global call for justice, resonating with countless individuals who courageously shared their own stories. The emotional weight of these narratives, along with a collective acknowledgment of a widespread problem, helped the movement gain incredible traction.

The impact of #MeToo has been immense, shaking up various industries and sparking discussions around consent, power dynamics, and accountability. This shows not only the potential for positive social change but also highlights how ideas can bring people together. The speed at which movements like this can rise emphasizes the importance of critically examining the content we engage with and the beliefs we support.

As we navigate this fast-moving world of information exchange, it's clear that viral ideas influence not just individual beliefs and actions but also shape societal norms, cultural conversations, and even policies. It's vital that we approach the information we come across online with thoughtfulness. Understanding how ideas are shared and amplified equips us to engage more mindfully with the digital landscape.

This understanding also calls for a commitment to critical thinking—actively questioning the ideas we encounter and the motivations driving them. In a time where ideas can spread rapidly, we each bear the responsibility to engage with information thoughtfully. As we wrestle with the implications of rapid idea sharing, we must create a culture that values truth, promotes understanding, and encourages constructive discussions.

By exploring how ideas spread quickly, the risks of misinformation, and the strength of viral movements, we can better appreciate the impact of our interactions with the online world. The ideas we support have the power to shape our lives, influence our communities, and ultimately direct the course of society. As we move forward in this new era, we must remain aware of the viral nature of ideas and the significant responsibilities that come with sharing them.

Understanding the complexities of how ideas spread today requires a mix of curiosity, critical thinking, and a genuine desire to grasp the stories that shape our world. Every time we come across a new idea, we face a choice: to share it and amplify it or to pause and consider its implications. The stakes are high, and the power is in our hands. As we engage with this ever-changing landscape of thought, let's be mindful of the ideas we choose to support, as they can either light the way toward progress or deepen the divides that hinder understanding and connection. The speed of modern virality deserves our attention, our responsibility, and ultimately, our action.

Peter Whitmore

Chapter 2: Anatomy of a Contagious Idea

Characteristics of Viral Ideas

In a world where ideas spread faster than ever, it's clear that some concepts strike a deeper chord than others. But what causes this difference? Why do certain ideas leap out from the shadows to capture global attention, while others fade away like forgotten treasures in a dusty attic? To understand this, we need to look at the qualities that make ideas not just memorable but also contagious.

First and foremost, relatability is at the heart of what makes an idea infectious. When an idea reflects our own experiences, challenges, or dreams, it creates an instant connection. Think about it: when we hear a story that feels familiar, we naturally nod along, feeling a bond with the person sharing it. These shared experiences act as bridges, helping us cross the sometimes intimidating gap between ourselves and the idea. This connection is both emotional and ideological. A relatable idea doesn't just resonate personally; it taps into what we all feel as part of our society.

Take the booming "self-care" movement as an example. With its focus on mindfulness, wellness, and mental health, this idea resonated with many people struggling under the constant pressure of modern life. It became relatable because it highlighted the truth that we all need to take care of ourselves amidst the chaos. As people began sharing their own self-care tips and routines, the concept didn't just spread; it evolved to fit everyone's unique needs. This shared understanding built a community that fully embraced the idea, allowing it to weave itself into our cultural story.

Emotional resonance is another key ingredient of viral ideas. Concepts that spark strong emotions—be it joy, anger, nostalgia, or empathy—tend to stick with us. Emotions act as powerful catalysts, pushing ideas from just thoughts to shared experiences. When an idea stirs up a strong reaction, it ignites a fire in us, driving us to share it with others. This sharing isn't just a passive act; it becomes a lively expression of our feelings, a way to connect with those around us.

Consider the impact of recent social movements like Black Lives Matter or Me Too. These movements have drawn on emotionally charged stories that highlight injustice, inequality, and the urgent need for change. These ideas resonated with people who could no longer stay silent about their own experiences with discrimination or harassment. By channeling their pain and anger into a collective voice, these movements transformed personal struggles into a shared belief system, creating a ripple effect that inspired widespread action and unity.

Simplicity also plays a crucial role in how ideas go viral. In a world flooded with information, clear and straightforward ideas are much easier to understand and embrace than complicated ones. Our brains have a limited capacity for processing information, so when we're bombarded with concepts, we naturally gravitate toward those that are simple. Easy-to-understand ideas can be quickly shared, turning into catchphrases that people repeat, slogans that echo, and messages that appear on protest signs.

Think about the powerful phrase "Black Lives Matter." This simple yet profound statement captures a complex social issue in just a few words. It serves as a rallying cry with immense power, conveying urgency and importance. Its straightforwardness makes it easy to share, adapt, and weave into conversations, transforming it from a mere idea into a movement that crosses geographic and cultural boundaries. The clarity of this message allows people from diverse backgrounds to unite behind it, amplifying its significance in public discussions.

Relevance is another crucial factor in spreading ideas. An idea that connects to current events, cultural shifts, or technological advancements is much more likely to catch on than one that feels outdated or irrelevant. As social beings, our beliefs are often shaped by the world around us. Ideas that address pressing concerns or resonate with popular sentiments are more likely to be shared and talked about.

For instance, during the COVID-19 pandemic, the idea of remote work became not just relevant but essential. With lockdowns forcing companies to adapt, the notion of working from home quickly shifted from being a rare option to the new standard. This sudden relevance thrust the idea into the spotlight, as people shared their experiences, tips, and challenges with this new way of working. Because it was so relevant, the idea wasn't just accepted; it was celebrated, sparking discussions about work-life balance and flexibility in the workplace.

These qualities—relatability, emotional resonance, simplicity, and relevance—work together to create an environment where ideas can thrive. Yet, the real magic happens when they unite in a compelling narrative. Much like a talented storyteller can captivate an audience with vivid imagery and relatable characters, a contagious idea flourishes when it's surrounded by engaging stories.

Storytelling is, in many ways, the backbone of an idea's ability to go viral. A well-told story can turn an abstract concept into a lively experience that jumps off the page and sticks in people's minds. This is where the power of storytelling meets the qualities of viral ideas. When an idea is wrapped in a story that embodies relatability, emotion, simplicity, and relevance, it becomes something truly powerful.

Look at the rise of the "sharing economy," represented by companies like Airbnb and Uber. These concepts didn't just emerge as business models; they became narratives about community, accessibility, and innovation. Every time someone shares their experience of staying in a home instead of a hotel or taking a ride from a stranger, they add to the story of how these platforms are transforming our social interactions and economic landscape. The narrative of empowerment and connection embedded in the sharing economy makes the idea not just memorable but highly contagious.

Moreover, we can't overlook the role of social media in spreading ideas today. Platforms like Twitter, Instagram, and TikTok have changed how we share and consume information. The ability to instantly share ideas with a global audience has created a fertile ground for contagious concepts. Social media acts as a loudspeaker, amplifying the characteristics we've discussed and providing a platform for narratives to grow and thrive.

The recent trend of viral challenges on platforms like TikTok is a perfect example of this. Challenges like the "Ice Bucket Challenge" or the "Mannequin Challenge" turned simple actions into widespread movements, engaging millions of users around the world. These challenges tapped into relatability, emotional engagement, and simplicity, allowing people to join in a shared experience that often had a meaningful cause behind it. The ease of sharing these challenges, combined with the stories that formed around them, helped propel them into the world of viral ideas.

As we think about what makes ideas contagious, it's clear they interact in a delicate dance. Relatability and emotional resonance build connections, simplicity ensures everyone can grasp them, and relevance keeps ideas grounded in today's reality. When these elements come together with powerful storytelling, it creates a fertile space for ideas to flourish.

The stories we share, the feelings we express, and the experiences we connect to are all threads in the intricate fabric of our social lives. Therefore, as we navigate the complexities of our increasingly interconnected world, understanding these qualities can give us an edge. By recognizing what makes ideas contagious, we can become more thoughtful consumers of information and better communicators of our own ideas.

In this time of information overload, where each click, like, and share can either spotlight an idea or push it into obscurity, it's vital that we engage meaningfully with the concepts that shape our lives. Being able to identify which ideas have the potential to go viral is more than just an intellectual exercise;

it's an important skill for anyone looking to understand the currents of modern culture. As we explore the dynamics of how ideas spread, it becomes clear that the landscape of beliefs, opinions, and ideologies is not just a passive background but a vibrant and evolving story that invites us all to take part.

The Role of Storytelling

Storytelling is as old as humanity, woven into the very essence of our lives. From the simple cave paintings of our ancestors to the grand tales of ancient civilizations, storytelling has always been a way for us to communicate, connect, and understand one another. Through stories, we make sense of the world around us, express our values, and share our beliefs. It's more than just entertainment; storytelling is a powerful tool that shapes our thoughts and influences society.

At the center of every great story is a well-told narrative. Classic story structures, like the hero's journey, help us grasp complex ideas and messages. This concept, made popular by Joseph Campbell, describes a hero who goes on an adventure, faces challenges, and comes back changed. This framework can be incredibly helpful when we want to share our ideas in a persuasive way.

Picture a young woman named Maya, who dreams of becoming an environmental scientist. As she looks at the mountains of plastic waste in her community, she feels a strong sense of urgency. Her journey begins when she goes to a local town hall meeting, where she discovers a grassroots movement aimed at reducing pollution. Despite facing pushback from those who don't see the value in her efforts, she becomes more determined than ever. The turning point comes when she leads a campaign that not only raises awareness but also gains community support, ultimately resulting in new recycling initiatives. Maya's story, told through the lens of the hero's journey, highlights the struggle between protecting the environment and societal indifference, sparking a larger conversation about sustainability.

The magic of this structure is in how it resonates with us. When we hear about Maya's struggles and victories, we can't help but feel emotionally connected to her journey. This connection allows us to engage more deeply with the important idea of environmental responsibility. In this way, the hero's journey becomes more than just a plot; it evolves into a way to convey critical truths about our society.

Creating characters we can relate to is another key part of storytelling. Characters act as bridges for ideas, helping us see ourselves in their stories. When we meet characters who evoke our empathy, we're more likely to engage with the thoughts they represent. There are many real-life examples where people have become symbols of larger movements through their personal tales.

Take Malala Yousafzai, for instance. This young Pakistani activist's story is a powerful testament to the fight for girls' education. She embodies courage, resilience, and determination. After surviving an assassination attempt by the Taliban, Malala's story crossed borders, capturing the hearts and minds of millions. Her journey turned a complex issue into something that feels real and relatable. Through her experiences, we are encouraged to reflect on our own views about education, gender equality, and activism.

Characters like Malala are vital because they help make abstract issues feel personal. When we read about the struggle for education, it's no longer just a statistic or a distant problem; it becomes an urgent issue involving real people with authentic struggles. These characters invite us into their experiences, allowing us to see the world through their eyes. By doing this, they amplify the ideas they represent and inspire others to join the fight.

Conflict is the heartbeat of storytelling, creating tension that keeps us engaged. When conflict is present, it raises the stakes, making both the story and its message more gripping. Whether it's an internal struggle or an external challenge, we pay closer attention. We become invested in how characters face their difficulties and eager to see how things unfold.

Take Rosa Parks, for example. She ignited the civil rights movement by refusing to give up her seat on a segregated bus. This act of defiance is rooted in deep conflict—not only her personal battle against systemic racism but also the larger fight for equality. The tension created by her decision, her arrest, and the ensuing boycott of the Montgomery bus system all underscore this larger conflict.

Rosa Parks' story shows how narratives filled with strong conflicts can shine a light on crucial ideas. The civil rights movement gained traction because it was woven with stories of struggle and resolution. Each act of defiance became a part of the rich narrative surrounding the fight for justice, inviting people to engage with the broader idea of equality.

Furthermore, storytelling is heavily influenced by cultural context. Different cultures tell and interpret stories in their own unique ways, affecting how ideas are embraced. Cultural archetypes and narratives can shape our understanding and acceptance of concepts, enriching the framework that informs how we interact with the world.

For instance, when we look at heroism, it's clear that various cultures have different takes. In many Western tales, the hero often symbolizes individualism and overcoming adversity. On the flip side, many Eastern stories highlight the importance of community and selflessness. This distinction is crucial when we think about how ideas are shared across cultures. A story that resonates strongly in one culture may not hold the same power in another, highlighting the need to understand the cultural perspectives through which we view ideas.

In our globally connected world, the blend of diverse narratives creates a rich space for ideas to thrive. But it also calls for sensitivity and awareness of cultural differences. When crafting a story, being mindful of these cultural nuances can enhance its effectiveness and reach. Stories that respect local traditions and values are more likely to connect with specific audiences, allowing the ideas they hold to flourish.

As we think about how storytelling shapes the spread of ideas, it becomes clear that elements like structure, relatable characters, conflict, and cultural context work together to weave compelling narratives. A well-told story can elevate an idea, transforming it from a simple thought into an experience that engages and inspires others.

In our digital age, where information spreads like wildfire, storytelling has taken on a whole new life. Social media and the internet have opened the floodgates for sharing stories, allowing ideas to travel faster than ever. The act of sharing personal narratives has empowered individuals to bring attention to important issues, amplifying voices in ways we never thought possible.

Look at the impact of viral hashtags on platforms like Twitter and Instagram. Movements such as #MeToo and #BlackLivesMatter gained momentum not just because of the ideas they stand for, but also through the powerful stories shared by individuals. These hashtags became vehicles for personal narratives that highlighted systemic injustices, resonating with audiences far and wide. By sharing their experiences, individuals contributed to a larger dialogue, inviting others to connect with the ideas behind these movements.

The storytelling we see on social media often embodies the qualities that make ideas contagious: relatability, emotional depth, simplicity, and relevance. When people share their stories, they tap into a shared experience, inviting others to connect and engage. The ease of sharing narratives creates a ripple effect, turning personal tales into collective movements that challenge societal norms and inspire change.

Ultimately, being able to craft effective narratives is a skill that benefits both personal and professional communication. Whether you're advocating for a cause, pitching a new idea, or simply sharing a personal experience, the way you tell your story can make a world of difference. By using storytelling principles, individuals can elevate their ideas, making them more relatable and powerful.

As we navigate the complexities of our interconnected world, it's more important than ever to recognize the power of storytelling. By honing our skills in crafting resonant narratives, we can contribute to the ongoing conversations about the ideas that shape our lives. In a world filled with noise, the stories we choose to share have the power to break through barriers, foster connections, and spark meaningful dialogues that inspire change. Through storytelling, we can bring our ideas to life, allowing them to thrive and connect with the hearts and minds of others.

Case Studies of Viral Concepts

Ideas can take on a life of their own, spreading quickly and igniting passions, movements, and conversations that truly change our society. The magic behind a viral idea is that it goes beyond just being a thought; it resonates deeply with people, stirring emotions, challenging the status quo, and even motivating collective action. As we dive into various case studies of viral concepts, we'll discover the key elements that make them so infectious—showing how storytelling, simplicity, and emotional appeal are vital to transforming an idea into a cultural phenomenon.

Let's kick things off with the viral sensation that took social media by storm in

2014: the Ice Bucket Challenge. It started as a simple concept—encouraging people to pour a bucket of ice water over themselves to support charity. Participants either took the chilly plunge or donated to the ALS Association, an organization dedicated to fighting amyotrophic lateral sclerosis, a serious neurodegenerative disease. Before long, the challenge became a worldwide movement, attracting celebrities, athletes, and everyday people alike.

So, what made the Ice Bucket Challenge so contagious? For one, the straightforward nature of the challenge made it easy for anyone to join in. All you needed was a bucket, some ice, and water. This simplicity broke down barriers, allowing people from all backgrounds to take part. But beyond being easy to do, the emotional aspect of the challenge was striking. It was about much more than just getting soaked; it was a heartfelt effort to shine a light on a disease many people were unaware of. The challenge became a unifying call for those affected by ALS and their families, creating emotional ties that went beyond just a splash of ice water.

We can't ignore the role of storytelling in the Ice Bucket Challenge's success. As videos flooded social media, personal narratives began to unfold. Participants started sharing their own experiences with ALS, turning those videos into moving testimonials. When public figures like Oprah Winfrey and Bill Gates took part, they didn't just join the fun; they helped amplify the challenge's message to millions. Their personal connections to the cause made it more relatable and inspired others to share their own stories.

The impact of the Ice Bucket Challenge was simply incredible. Within just a few months, the ALS Association reported raising over $115 million—a dramatic spike from the $19 million raised in the same period the previous year. Those funds enabled important research and support for individuals living with ALS. Not only did the challenge raise money, but it also significantly boosted awareness about the disease, encouraging more conversations about its impact. The Ice Bucket Challenge set an example for how social media can be used for good, inspiring many other campaigns that aimed to replicate its success.

Another example of a viral concept is the "Share a Coke" campaign launched by Coca-Cola in 2011. The idea was straightforward: swap out Coca-Cola's iconic logo for some of the most popular names, encouraging people to find bottles featuring their names or those of friends and family. This simple twist on personalization completely changed how consumers interacted with the brand.

There are several reasons why "Share a Coke" became so popular. For one, it tapped into our natural desire for personal connection. By placing names on the bottles, Coca-Cola created a sense of ownership and individuality. The product felt special, and consumers were excited to share their find with their friends. The thrill of spotting one's name on a bottle sparked a wave of excitement, with people rushing to discover bottles that featured their names or those of loved ones.

Storytelling played a huge role in the campaign too. Coca-Cola cleverly crafted narratives around the idea of sharing. Advertisements showed friends and family gathering with their personalized bottles, evoking feelings of happiness and togetherness. The campaign encouraged people to share their experiences on social media with the hashtag #ShareaCoke, creating a shared narrative focused on the joy of connection. These personal stories, combined with eye-catching visuals of the customized bottles, deepened the emotional investment in the campaign.

The results were impressive. The campaign led to a significant boost in Coca-Cola's sales, with more than 500,000 photos shared on social media in just the first year. It became a cultural phenomenon, sparking discussions about connection and the importance of community. The success of "Share a Coke" shows how a campaign that combines simplicity, emotional engagement, and storytelling can generate widespread interest and ultimately drive consumer behavior.

Grassroots movements also provide powerful examples of how ideas can gather momentum and reshape societal conversations. The "Black Lives Matter" movement arose in response to the systemic injustices faced by Black individuals in the United States, fueled by heartbreaking incidents of police violence. What began as a hashtag quickly grew into a global movement, capturing many of the qualities that make concepts go viral.

At its core, Black Lives Matter is a clear and impactful call to action. The phrase itself resonates with many who have felt marginalized or oppressed. The movement is significant not just for its name but also for the deep-rooted issues it addresses. It embodies the feelings of anger, frustration, and hope that countless individuals around the world carry. This emotional drive creates a sense of urgency for people to get involved, sparking discussions about race, justice, and equality.

Storytelling has played a crucial role in amplifying the message of Black Lives Matter. Each incident of police violence against Black individuals—such as the tragic deaths of Trayvon Martin, Michael Brown, and George Floyd—has sparked collective outrage and led to powerful narratives that highlight the human cost of systemic racism. These stories, often shared on social media, serve as reminders of the ongoing struggles faced by the Black community and the urgent need for change. By weaving personal stories with broader historical themes, the movement creates a compelling narrative that urges society to reflect and act.

The impact of the Black Lives Matter movement has been significant, raising awareness about racial injustices and prompting discussions in boardrooms, classrooms, and homes worldwide. It has inspired protests, influenced policy changes, and caused a reassessment of systemic racism in various institutions. Additionally, the movement has sparked a wave of other social initiatives, encouraging people to speak up against injustice and advocate for change in their own communities.

All of these case studies highlight how certain ideas can go viral through a mix of simplicity, emotional resonance, and compelling storytelling. The Ice Bucket Challenge turned a charitable effort into a cultural phenomenon, Coca-Cola's "Share a Coke" campaign connected personal experiences with consumer engagement, and the Black Lives Matter movement has opened essential dialogues about race and justice on a global scale.

By examining these concepts, we can start to understand the intricate dynamics that allow ideas to spread. These case studies show that when ideas resonate emotionally and are presented through relatable narratives, they can reach far beyond their original intentions, creating movements and conversations that shape our society.

In a world overflowing with information, recognizing what makes ideas go viral can help us engage more thoughtfully with the narratives that surround us. Whether through social media challenges, marketing campaigns, or grassroots movements, the principles behind viral concepts provide a guide for understanding how ideas can capture attention, inspire action, and ultimately lead to positive change in our communities.

As we reflect on these case studies, think about how you might apply these insights to your own encounters with ideas that have moved you. What stories strike a chord with you? What movements motivate you to take action? The next time you come across a contagious idea, remember that its journey is built on emotional connections, simplicity, and the timeless art of storytelling. You have the power to recognize and amplify these narratives, whether in your own efforts or as part of something larger. By doing so, you contribute to the ongoing conversations about progress and change, ensuring that the ideas you value can inspire others just as they have inspired you.

Chapter 3: Psychological Susceptibility and Adoption

Cognitive Biases at Play

The mind is a fascinating thing, filled with thoughts and processes that shape how we see the world. Among the many aspects of human thinking, cognitive biases are particularly noteworthy. These biases aren't just odd quirks; they are consistent patterns that steer us away from logical reasoning. In a world where we are constantly bombarded with information, our brains use these mental shortcuts to help us sort through the overwhelming flow of ideas. While these shortcuts can make our thinking quicker, they can also lead us to make irrational decisions, causing us to believe things that may not be true.

One of the most intriguing biases we encounter is social proof. This bias works on the idea that we often look to others when deciding what to believe or how to act. The saying "if many people are doing it, it must be right" resonates deeply with us. As social creatures, we crave validation from those around us, especially in situations that feel new or uncertain. Studies show that social proof plays a role in everything from what we buy to how social movements gain traction. Take the example of a new restaurant opening up. If you walk by and see a line of hungry customers waiting to get in, you might think the food must be fantastic, even if you have no clue what the menu offers.

Social media has taken this bias to a whole new level. With just a click, ideas can spread quickly, often based more on how popular they are than on their actual value. A single tweet can spark a trending topic that sways public opinion, no matter how truthful it is. In echo chambers—those online spaces where people with similar views gather—social proof can create a bubble where certain ideas flourish simply because they resonate with the majority. The louder the agreement, the more likely others are to adopt those views.

A classic example of social proof in action can be found in viral challenges on social media, where users are encouraged to perform tasks and share their experiences. The Ice Bucket Challenge, which raised awareness for amyotrophic lateral sclerosis (ALS), illustrates this perfectly. As videos of people pouring ice water over themselves went viral, the massive participation turned a small cause into a widespread movement almost overnight. It wasn't rational thinking about the cause that drove this surge; it was the powerful influence of social proof. Everyone was involved, and that visibility made it seem like the right thing to do.

However, this collective behavior can also lead us to accept risky or misguided ideas. A stark example of this is the spread of misinformation on social media. When a false claim gets shared widely, many people start to believe it must be true simply because so many others are discussing it. This can cloud our ability to tell fact from fiction. Following the crowd can be comforting, but recognizing it as a bias is crucial to maintaining clear judgment.

Beyond social proof, there's another fascinating bias to consider: the impact of authority cues. We naturally tend to respect authority, and this respect can shape our beliefs and actions more than we realize. From a young age, we learn to listen to teachers, parents, and leaders, leading us to accept their guidance without much questioning. This respect for authority figures—whether they are experts, celebrities, or charismatic leaders—can sway public opinion and encourage us to adopt certain ideas, sometimes dangerously so.

For example, during the COVID-19 pandemic, public health officials became key authority figures for many. Their expertise was vital in steering us through an unprecedented crisis. However, authority can also have negative consequences. In politics, charismatic leaders can use their influence to promote ideologies that play into their followers' biases. A notable case is when a respected politician advocates for a specific health measure, like vaccinations. People are more likely to accept that belief just because of who is saying it. Conversely, if that same figure questions a health initiative, many may follow suit, ignoring scientific evidence and expert advice.

This situation raises important questions about the nature of authority and its role in shaping our beliefs. The line between genuine expertise and the misuse of that expertise is often very thin. Authority figures can inspire positive change and understanding, but they can also mislead and manipulate their followers' beliefs. It's crucial to recognize this bias as we navigate the many ideas we encounter daily.

Another bias that complicates how we adopt ideas is confirmation bias. Once we adopt a belief or ideology, confirmation bias kicks in, leading us to seek out information that supports our existing views. This can create an echo chamber in our minds, where we ignore any contradictory evidence and focus only on what aligns with our beliefs. The effects of confirmation bias can be significant; it limits our exposure to different perspectives and reinforces our ideologies, often resulting in a stubborn mindset that's hard to change.

Think about someone who strongly identifies with a particular political ideology. They might read news articles, follow social media influencers, and engage in discussions that reflect and validate their beliefs. When faced with evidence that contradicts their views, they may dismiss it or label it as "fake news." The comfort of being surrounded by like-minded individuals can feel great, but it can also stifle real growth and understanding.

There are countless stories of people grappling with confirmation bias in their personal and professional lives. For example, in business, decision-makers might cling to a failing strategy simply because it was their idea. When shown data that suggests they need to change course, they may reinterpret the information to suit their original vision. This not only hinders innovation but can also lead to significant losses for companies that refuse to adapt.

The relationship between confirmation bias and the digital age has only made this issue worse. Social media algorithms are designed to show us content that matches our interests, pushing us deeper into our ideological bubbles. The more we engage with content that confirms our preferences, the more we see similar material, reinforcing our beliefs without any challenge. This sets off a cycle that can perpetuate divisive ideologies and make genuine conversation difficult.

Understanding how cognitive biases work is critical for building a society that values critical thinking and open discussions. We need to be self-aware, recognizing when our biases might be clouding our judgment or limiting our perspective. By actively seeking out different viewpoints and challenging our own beliefs, we can break free from the grips of cognitive biases and engage more thoughtfully with the world.

Recognizing that cognitive biases exist is one thing; addressing them in our daily lives is another. The range of biases at play—social proof, authority cues, and confirmation bias— aren't just academic concepts; they are part of our reality. The next time you find yourself agreeing with an idea, take a moment to pause and reflect. Ask yourself: Am I going along with what everyone else thinks? Am I just following an authority figure without questioning? Am I only looking for information that confirms what I already believe?

These questions can lead to deeper understanding and personal growth. By openly engaging with our cognitive biases, we can become more thoughtful consumers of ideas. This process helps us critically assess the beliefs that shape our lives and our society, ultimately leading to a more compassionate and reflective human experience.

Emotional Triggers: The Heart's Influence on Ideology

Ideas and beliefs don't just live in our minds; they thrive in the emotions that connect us as people. This emotional world is vast, filled with a range of feelings like joy, fear, anger, and sadness. Each of these emotions has a huge impact on how we accept certain ideas and decide what we want to share with others. It's in this emotional space that we discover the real strength of persuasion.

Let's take a closer look at fear. This powerful emotion has often been used to manipulate people. The fear of the unknown can lead individuals to accept ideas they might not have considered otherwise. We see fear tactics everywhere—in politics, advertising, and even the news. When fear is stirred up, it creates a sense of urgency that makes people accept messages without really thinking them through. Think about election time: candidates often spotlight threats, whether they're real or exaggerated, to rally support and get voters behind their plans. The message is clear: "If you don't act now, bad things will happen."

There's a reason this tactic works: fear taps into a basic human instinct. Throughout history, fear helped our ancestors react quickly to dangers, increasing their chances of survival. Today, that same emotional response can sway our beliefs and actions. But there's a downside—fear can also cloud our judgment. When people are scared, they might ignore logical reasoning and instead cling to whatever narrative feels emotionally strongest.

An example of this was the global response to the COVID-19 pandemic. The rapid spread of the virus triggered widespread fear, leading many to adopt various opinions about health and safety measures. In this environment, misinformation spread easily as some turned to alternative stories that promised comfort or answers. Fear's intensity often drowns out calm, rational voices, leading to the acceptance of ideas that might deserve a second look.

On the flip side, joy can also be a powerful driver of ideas. Feeling joyful can make people more open to new experiences and concepts. Joy fosters a sense of community, encouraging individuals to embrace shared beliefs. Look at movements focused on positivity or social change, like environmental activism or community service—they frequently use joyful emotions to inspire involvement.

The feel-good nature of these movements can make ideas spread like wildfire. Social media campaigns often tap into joy, creating shareable content that invites others to join in simply because it feels good. When a touching video of a charitable act goes viral, it can motivate viewers to mimic those actions, sharing the idea widely without the need for deep thought.

However, while joy is uplifting, it can sometimes lead to shallow engagement with ideas. When feelings of happiness overshadow critical thinking, people might adopt beliefs without fully understanding them. So, it's crucial to find a balance between feeling and thinking. The challenge is to harness the power of joy while still engaging with ideas in a thoughtful way.

Anger, too, deserves attention. This strong emotion can be both a motivator and a hindrance. Anger can drive people to stand up for justice or challenge unfairness. Movements fueled by anger often gain momentum quickly, as shared frustration unites different groups around a common cause. For instance, the Black Lives Matter movement arose largely from anger about systemic racism, shining a light on social issues that demanded change. Anger can create solidarity among activists, helping new ideas that shake up the status quo gain acceptance.

Yet, like fear and joy, anger can also cloud our judgment. When people act out of anger, they may lose the ability to critically evaluate the ideas they embrace and promote. This intense emotion can lead to hasty actions and decisions that lack careful thought. For example, a furious post on social media can spark a heated response, but those conversations can quickly spiral out of control, drowning out more nuanced discussions in favor of catchy phrases and slogans.

Sadness is another emotion that can greatly influence how we accept ideas, though it often doesn't get as much attention. Sadness can spark empathy and compassion, moving individuals to support causes that resonate with them emotionally. When people encounter tragic situations, they often feel compelled to help and advocate for solutions to those issues. The weight of sadness can serve as a powerful motivation for action.

Think about how documentaries and charity campaigns depict human suffering. These stories are often crafted to evoke sadness, creating a strong emotional connection that encourages people to adopt beliefs that aim to reduce that suffering. Emotional storytelling can be a powerful motivator. When we witness the struggles of others, our emotional reactions can lead us to embrace ideas focused on kindness and change.

This relationship between emotion and ideology shows why it's important to recognize the emotional triggers that shape our beliefs. By understanding how emotions influence our openness to ideas, we can approach the complicated world of beliefs with more awareness. It's not just about what we believe; it's about how we feel about those beliefs that shapes how we accept and share them.

To navigate these emotional triggers wisely, we need to develop self-awareness. By recognizing the feelings involved in our decision-making, we can better understand why some ideas attract us while we dismiss others. This self-reflection helps us engage with our emotions thoughtfully, allowing us to question how they might be influencing our beliefs and interactions.

Storytelling is a fantastic way to deepen our grasp of emotional triggers. Sharing personal stories—whether our own or those of others—can shed light on how emotions drive our beliefs. By sharing experiences that evoke strong feelings, we can build connections that cross ideological boundaries.

In addition, conversations that prioritize emotional intelligence can help create a more empathetic society. By acknowledging the emotions that shape our discussions, we can foster spaces for genuine communication. These conversations can aid us in navigating the complexities of our emotional responses while encouraging understanding and acceptance of different beliefs.

As we explore the strong connection between emotional triggers and the beliefs we adopt, it becomes clear that our hearts play a crucial role in shaping how we think. Fear, joy, anger, and sadness are not just reactions; they are significant forces guiding our choices. Being aware of these emotional influences can empower us to engage with ideas thoughtfully, leading to richer conversations and a deeper understanding of one another.

The emotions that connect us are the same emotions that can set us apart. Being aware of these dynamics is key to navigating the variety of beliefs we encounter in our lives. By promoting emotional awareness and thoughtful engagement, we can learn to approach the ideologies we accept and share in a more reflective way. Ultimately, it's not just about the ideas themselves—it's the feelings they spark that genuinely shape our view of the world.

Identity and Belonging

Identity shapes how we see the world and influences how we interact with others, what we believe, and what ideas we accept or reject. Whether we realize it or not, our identities—formed by our ethnicity, religion, political beliefs, or other community ties—play a big role in our perspectives. They weave together our views, likes, and dislikes. Understanding the link between identity and the ideas we hold is key to grasping how certain thoughts become popular and spread quickly among those who feel connected to one another.

Social Identity Theory gives us a helpful way to think about this connection. This theory suggests that we define ourselves based on the groups we belong to. While this sense of identity can bring people together and create a sense of community, it can also lead to division and exclusion. The groups we associate with—whether they are based on religion, ethnicity, politics, or social interests—help form our beliefs and values. For example, research shows that people who strongly identify with a particular political party are more likely to support ideas that align with their party's beliefs, even if those ideas aren't backed by facts. This shows how group loyalty can cloud our judgment and affect how we see things.

Think about community organizing in social movements like the Civil Rights

Movement or modern environmental activism. In these cases, shared identity acts like fuel for collective beliefs. The fight for civil rights by the African American community wasn't just about legal rights; it was also a powerful assertion of their identity. Leaders like Martin Luther King Jr. used the common experiences and cultural identity of African Americans to rally support for their cause, leading to significant changes in beliefs throughout the country. Here, shared identity became a powerful motivator for collective action and for embracing ideas that challenged the traditional way of thinking.

However, while shared identities can inspire collective beliefs, they can also create a clear divide between those who are part of the group and those who aren't. These dynamics can make it hard for group members to consider new or different ideas. Groupthink is a common issue in this environment, where the desire for agreement leads to poor decision-making. When people prioritize harmony over critical thinking, they risk shutting down new ideas and reinforcing negative beliefs.

A clear example of this can be found in political discussions. When a political group is faced with ideas that challenge their usual beliefs—like a new economic policy that contradicts what they have always thought—the members might oppose it not because it's a bad idea, but because it threatens the unity of their group. This can result in dismissing facts and evidence, as sticking to group norms becomes more important. The pressure to go along with the group can create an echo chamber, where alternative viewpoints are ignored, and different opinions are pushed aside, further deepening unhelpful beliefs.

The role of community in shaping shared beliefs is incredibly important. Communities act as environments where values and beliefs are created and nurtured. Whether they are religious groups, cultural communities, or social clubs, these environments help form collective identities, reinforcing shared beliefs through common practices and stories. For example, religious groups often have rich traditions and teachings that continually affirm their members' beliefs. The feeling of belonging that comes from being part of such communities can bring comfort and stability, but it can also create a rigid way of thinking that limits personal growth and change in beliefs.

Consider a close-knit religious group. Members often absorb the teachings and beliefs shared within their community, creating a strong bond. Yet, this same bond can also lead to excluding ideas from outside the group—ideas that could enhance or challenge their understanding. The danger here is that people might become so tied to their community's identity that they avoid other viewpoints, effectively narrowing their perspectives.

Still, in our more connected world, identity isn't as fixed as it used to be. The idea of identity fluidity suggests that people can navigate multiple identities that shift and change over time. This idea brings both challenges and opportunities for embracing new thoughts. As individuals deal with the complexities of their identities—especially in diverse settings—they often come across different viewpoints that can inspire changes in their beliefs.

Take immigrants, for example. They often find themselves balancing two cultures. They may feel a sense of belonging to their ethnic community while also trying to fit into the broader society. This dual existence can lead them to develop hybrid identities, allowing them to embrace multiple viewpoints. As they navigate these identities, they may become more open to ideas that they wouldn't have considered if they were only focused on their original community. This flexibility can encourage innovation and new ways of thinking, enabling individuals to challenge what they thought they knew and welcome new ideas.

Moreover, in today's social media age, the ways our identities and sense of belonging are shaped have changed even more. Online communities let people connect with others who share their interests and beliefs, no matter where they live. This virtual world can create new in-groups, where ideas can spread quickly among those who feel a connection. However, this can also lead to division as people tailor their online experiences to fit their beliefs, making it easier to stick with what they already think. The rapid spread of ideas on social media highlights the need to understand how identity influences the sharing of thoughts.

As we look more closely at how identity affects the acceptance of ideas, it's clear that belonging is crucial in shaping our beliefs. The desire for social connection and acceptance can push people toward ideologies that feel right for them. Yet, this same need can also lead to excluding those who think differently, making it harder to think critically and innovate.

The connection between identity and ideology shows why we need to be mindful of the beliefs we choose to embrace. By acknowledging the role our identities play in shaping how we see things, we can approach new ideas with more thoughtfulness. Promoting conversations that bridge gaps and challenge the status quo can help us develop a broader understanding of different belief systems.

In the end, the complex relationship between identity and belonging shows us that our beliefs don't form in isolation. They're shaped by the groups we're part of, the communities we live in, and the identities we adopt. Understanding this relationship empowers us to navigate the world of ideas more thoughtfully, encouraging a more open-minded and compassionate society. It invites us to question the stories we accept and to engage thoughtfully with the wide range of perspectives that shape our lives.

Peter Whitmore

Chapter 4: Networks—the Highways of Ideological Spread

The Structure of Social Networks

Picture a vast web sparkling in the light, full of connections visible and hidden. Each thread symbolizes a relationship, a link, a flow of ideas and information. This isn't just a fancy way to describe how we interact; it's a peek into what makes up social networks, which are like highways for sharing thoughts and beliefs. These networks are woven into the very core of how we connect with one another, representing the complex and often messy relationships between people, communities, and the information that bounces around between them.

At the center of any social network are nodes and edges. Nodes are the people—each one unique, filled with their own thoughts, feelings, and perspectives. Edges represent the connections between these people—friends, acquaintances, coworkers, family members, and even those we've just met. The dance between these nodes and edges is what allows ideas to flow and spread. Just like a road system needs streets and intersections for cars to move around, our social fabric needs these connections to let ideas navigate through society.

To really understand how ideas spread, it's helpful to see the different models that show how these networks can be set up. One of the most interesting models is the small-world network. Imagine a huge group of people linked by tight-knit circles. Inside these circles, people know each other well, sharing thoughts and experiences closely. What makes small-world networks so captivating is their ability to connect different clusters through a few key individuals—often called "hubs." These hubs can quickly spread ideas across faraway groups, illustrating how just one strong connection can change the whole network's direction.

A powerful example of a small-world network in action is the civil rights movement in the United States during the 1960s. Activists, often linked through local groups, worked hard to spread messages of equality and justice. Thanks to the efforts of a few influential leaders and organizers, these messages reached far beyond their immediate friends and family, touching broader audiences and sparking significant social change. The ripple effect of their ideas shows how small-world networks can help powerful concepts grow into real movements.

In contrast, we have scale-free networks, which work differently. Here, the connections aren't evenly spread out. Instead, a small number of people have a lot of connections, while most have just a few. This leads to a power-law distribution, where some people get more connected over time. In real life, this means certain individuals or organizations become key players in sharing ideas because of their many connections. Think of social media influencers—when they post something, their huge follower base can share it widely, spreading ideas faster than ever before.

To understand this better, think about how public health information spread during the COVID-19 pandemic. Central figures like healthcare officials, hospitals, and government agencies acted as nodes with many connections. When they shared important information— like safety tips, vaccination updates, or new research—these well-connected entities allowed the information to flow through various social circles, often reaching those who might not have direct contact with the sources. This shows how the structure of social networks helps ensure that vital information spreads quickly and influences public behavior and attitudes.

In the world of ideas, the layout of social networks isn't just a background setting; it plays an active role. The paths created by these networks determine how quickly and effectively new ideas can spread. These interconnected structures allow for the quick sharing of thoughts, leading to significant changes in societal norms and behaviors.

Surprisingly, social networks aren't just a product of human interaction; they reflect patterns seen in nature and technology. For example, think about how neurons connect in the human brain or how the internet is structured. Both systems rely on nodes and edges to share information, highlighting the universal significance of these basic elements. Whether it's helping people communicate or sending data across digital channels, the core ideas remain the same.

However, just having a network doesn't automatically mean ideas will spread successfully. The way people interact within that network matters too. Some individuals act as bridges between different groups, while others might stick closely to their own circle. How willing people are to share, discuss, and promote ideas is what really determines how effective the network is at spreading concepts. This willingness is influenced by many factors, including trust, social connections, and group dynamics.

As we move through our connected lives, it's vital to think about the structure of social networks. Recognizing that we're not just passive receivers of ideas but active players in the exchange can inspire us to engage more thoughtfully with the information we encounter. Every conversation we have, each social media interaction, and all the connections we build play a part in the larger network of ideas swirling around us.

Now that we understand social networks as channels for sharing ideas, let's take a moment to think about the role of "weak ties" in this process. While we often focus on sharing ideas with our close friends and family, it's often those more casual connections that help ideas reach beyond our immediate circles. These weak ties serve as bridges to new networks, broadening the impact of concepts and ensuring that ideas don't get stuck within familiar boundaries.

The Power of Weak Ties

At first, the idea of weak ties might seem a bit strange. When we think about the connections that matter most to us, we often picture our closest friends and family—those people we share strong bonds with. But surprisingly, it's those looser connections—like acquaintances, coworkers, or even brief encounters with strangers—that can be incredibly powerful when it comes to sharing ideas and information. Mark Granovetter's groundbreaking study, particularly his influential work "The Strength of Weak Ties," shows how these weaker links can act as crucial pathways for the flow of knowledge through our social networks.

Granovetter's research challenges the common belief that our strongest relationships provide the most significant benefits. Instead, he suggests that it's often our weaker ties that open up new doors to fresh opportunities, different viewpoints, and innovative ideas. Think about your close friends; chances are they share similar backgrounds and experiences with you. Because of this, the conversations you have with them might often cover the same ground, repeatedly bouncing around familiar ideas. On the other hand, weak ties connect us to a wider range of social circles, exposing us to new information and perspectives we might not encounter otherwise.

Take, for example, the dynamic world of Silicon Valley, a true hotbed for innovation and entrepreneurship. Here, the influence of weak ties is unmistakable. Startups don't just thrive because talented individuals are working closely together; they also flourish because those individuals are part of a broader web of contacts. Entrepreneurs frequently meet potential collaborators, investors, and mentors in the most surprising places—at networking events, through casual introductions, or even during random encounters at coffee shops. These weak ties can ignite groundbreaking ideas and lead to collaborative projects that simply wouldn't have happened within a tight-knit group.

A great example of this is the tech startup culture in Silicon Valley, where people from vastly different backgrounds come together to share and refine their ideas. Imagine a programmer meeting a marketer at a networking event, leading to the creation of a groundbreaking app that neither would have thought of alone. Each person brings their unique insights, experiences, and connections, creating a rich environment for innovation to thrive. This blending of ideas is exactly what weak ties encourage, expanding our understanding of what's possible.

Moreover, weak ties play a significant role in enriching creativity and diverse thinking. When we interact with people outside our usual circles, we gain exposure to different opinions, experiences, and thought processes. This kind of exposure can spark new ideas and fuel innovation. Research shows that having diverse perspectives leads to better problem-solving and more creative results. In many creative fields, from design to software development, the most groundbreaking innovations often emerge from the blending of varied ideas. Weak ties help bridge these differences, encouraging us to think outside the box and challenge the norm.

The impact of weak ties goes beyond technology and creativity; they also play a vital role in public health communication. During crises, like the Ebola outbreak or the COVID-19 pandemic, getting vital information out to the public quickly and effectively is crucial. Interestingly, individuals who aren't in regular contact with healthcare professionals can still receive important health messages through their weak ties. Picture a community member learning about vaccination updates or safety protocols from a coworker or neighbor rather than from a doctor. These weak ties can be instrumental in spreading public health messages to groups that might not otherwise hear them, effectively filling gaps in knowledge.

During the Ebola outbreak, health officials quickly understood the value of tapping into community networks for communication. They encouraged local leaders, often seen as trusted figures, to share information about the disease and prevention methods. By using these weak ties, officials could reach people who might not have trusted traditional health communications. This strategy allowed information to flow more freely through social networks, ultimately helping to control the outbreak.

The COVID-19 pandemic further highlighted the importance of weak ties in health communication. As the virus spread rapidly worldwide, public health agencies faced the daunting challenge of informing everyone about safety measures, vaccine distribution, and risk reduction. Social media became a vital tool for sharing information, allowing people to update their wider networks with personal stories, tips, and advice. The information shared by acquaintances often felt more relatable and resonated more deeply than official announcements, proving once again how weak ties can effectively connect formal institutions with the general public.

The effectiveness of weak ties in spreading information isn't limited to health communication; it's a recurring theme throughout history. Think about how weak ties were essential during the civil rights movement and other social movements. Activists relied on acquaintances to spread the word about protests, rallies, and initiatives. These weak ties were key in rallying people who might not have been actively involved. By reaching into the broader social fabric, movements could amplify their messages and inspire widespread participation.

Additionally, weak ties also shape behavior. Research suggests that people are more likely to adopt behaviors endorsed by acquaintances rather than close friends or family. This can happen because we often seek social validation; we may be influenced by those on the edges of our social circles since they give the impression that a certain behavior is acceptable or common. For instance, someone might be more inclined to try a new fitness class after hearing about it from a coworker rather than from a close friend who goes to the same gym. Weak ties create chances for social learning, encouraging us to step out of our comfort zones and embrace new experiences.

In our digital age, the influence of weak ties has evolved significantly thanks to technology. Social media platforms connect people who might not have met otherwise. A tweet or Facebook post can reach hundreds or even thousands of individuals, often including acquaintances who share an interest in a specific topic. This digital landscape enables ideas and information to spread quickly, making weak ties more powerful than ever.

However, it's important to keep in mind that weak ties can have both positive and negative effects. While they can be channels for sharing innovative ideas and necessary information, they can also unintentionally contribute to the spread of misinformation. With information so easily accessible online, there's a greater risk of misunderstandings, exaggerations, or even outright falsehoods. When acquaintances share sensational stories or unverified claims, the consequences can be significant. The viral nature of social media means that misinformation can quickly spread through weak ties, causing confusion or harmful actions.

This dual nature of weak ties—their ability to share fresh ideas while also posing the risk of spreading misinformation—highlights the need for us to think critically about the information we consume and share. While weak ties can introduce us to new viewpoints, we must also evaluate the credibility of the information flowing through these networks. Engaging with a variety of perspectives is vital, but so is ensuring that the ideas we promote are backed by solid evidence and trustworthy sources.

In the end, recognizing the power of weak ties can change how we navigate our lives. By intentionally nurturing these loose connections, we can build a network that encourages innovation, creativity, and the sharing of valuable information. In our increasingly interconnected world, every interaction with an acquaintance is an opportunity to broaden our horizons and deepen our understanding of the world. Whether it's through casual chats at the grocery store or conversations on social media, our weak ties can unlock new ideas and inspire meaningful change.

As we consider the importance of weak ties, it becomes clear that they are not just small details in the story of human connection. Instead, they are vital threads that enrich our social fabric. By understanding and embracing the power of these connections, we can use them to venture into new realms of thought, collaboration, and innovation.

Digital Platforms as Accelerators

In the fast-changing digital landscape we find ourselves in today, social media platforms serve as powerful engines that bring ideas from the hidden corners of the internet into the public eye. The algorithms behind these platforms act like a digital megaphone, amplifying some voices while muting others. This creates interesting questions about what we see and how we process information. How does a simple hashtag or a viral challenge manage to captivate so many people? Why do some ideas go viral while others quickly fade away?

Let's take a moment to reflect on the #MeToo movement, which fundamentally changed how we talk about sexual harassment and assault. This movement is a prime example of how social media can fuel social change. When actress Alyssa Milano encouraged people to share their experiences with the hashtag, it sparked a global conversation that went far beyond its initial moment. Suddenly, countless stories came together, forming a powerful narrative that demanded accountability and reform. Each retweet and share acted like a connection in a vast web, linking people from different backgrounds and experiences, and giving strength to a shared cause.

Another striking example is the Black Lives Matter movement, which utilized social media's power to confront systemic racism and police brutality. This movement started with a tweet following the acquittal of George Zimmerman in the tragic death of Trayvon Martin. It quickly grew, fueled by hashtags that became rallying cries for justice. The digital world became a hub for organizing protests, sharing resources, and elevating the voices of those who are often overlooked. By fostering a sense of urgency and unity, these platforms not only helped spread ideas but also mobilized people around the globe, showcasing their unique ability to ignite social movements.

However, while these platforms can drive positive change, they have a darker side that can lead to division and the spread of misinformation. The algorithms that prioritize engaging content often favor sensational or emotionally charged posts, which can distort public discussions and create echo chambers. In these echo chambers, people find themselves wrapped in a bubble of similar opinions. The result is a space where confirmation bias thrives; individuals mainly encounter ideas that reinforce their existing beliefs. This isn't just a theoretical issue; it has serious effects on how society deals with complex topics and differing opinions.

Think about the 2016 U.S. presidential election, which starkly highlighted the consequences of these echo chambers driven by algorithms. Voters online were often bombarded with tailored content that matched their biases, leading to deeper divisions within our society. The very algorithms designed to maximize engagement ended up fueling an environment full of misinformation and extreme rhetoric. What began as a casual scroll through social media turned into a battleground for conflicting ideas. The fallout was significant, impacting not just politics but also the core of how we communicate with one another.

The effects of echo chambers reach beyond politics. In public health, misinformation can spread just as rapidly. During the COVID-19 pandemic, the digital space became flooded with conflicting information about vaccines, treatments, and safety protocols. With reliable sources hard to find, many turned to their social networks—often made up of casual acquaintances—to find the truth. This reliance on personal connections for information, while understandable, created a ripe environment for false narratives to thrive. The spread of conspiracy theories and unfounded claims highlighted the urgent need to think critically about the information we consume.

So, what responsibilities do digital platforms have in this tricky landscape? As the gatekeepers of information, these companies have significant power in shaping public conversations. Many critics argue that platforms must actively manage content to prevent the spread of misinformation and hate speech. Yet, finding the right balance between freedom of expression and responsible moderation is a contentious issue. The algorithms that determine what we see can unintentionally suppress diverse opinions, creating an environment that stifles meaningful conversation.

Consider the decisions made by algorithms that led to the censorship of certain political content during heated election times. Critics have pointed out that platforms sometimes apply their policies inconsistently, raising ethical questions about who gets a voice, who gets listened to, and who gets silenced. In a time when a variety of perspectives is more important than ever, the duty of digital platforms to promote healthy public discourse cannot be overstated.

To tackle these challenges, several policy recommendations have surfaced to encourage more positive online conversations. First and foremost, transparency in how algorithms work is crucial. Understanding how algorithms decide what content to prioritize can empower users to engage thoughtfully with the ideas they come across. Additionally, platforms can support media literacy initiatives, equipping users with the skills to assess the credibility of information. Promoting digital literacy helps individuals distinguish fact from fiction and approach content with a more critical mindset.

Moreover, platforms should consider working alongside fact-checking organizations to verify the information shared on their sites.

By providing users with accurate context and reliable sources, digital platforms can take a proactive stance against misinformation. This collaborative approach not only nurtures healthier discourse but also enhances the platforms' reputation as responsible curators of information.

However, the responsibility for creating a healthy digital environment doesn't rest solely on tech companies. As information consumers, we also have a role in navigating this digital world. Being mindful of what we consume can lead to a richer understanding of our surroundings. This involves seeking out diverse viewpoints, questioning the information we come across, and engaging in discussions that challenge our own perspectives.

Engaging with differing opinions, even when it feels uncomfortable, can deepen our understanding of complex issues. When we encounter ideas that clash with our beliefs, we are given a chance to grow. By taking part in thoughtful dialogue, we contribute to a more nuanced discussion that goes beyond simple black-and-white thinking.

The digital age has changed the way we connect, share, and engage with ideas. Yet, with this power comes great responsibility. As we navigate this intricate web of information, it's crucial to stay alert to the dangers of echo chambers and misinformation. The choices we make about what we consume and how we interact with others can significantly influence the landscape of ideas around us.

Looking ahead, the potential for digital platforms to drive meaningful progress is enormous. By using their power wisely, we can create a healthier digital environment that encourages the exchange of diverse ideas and thoughtful discussions. In this way, we can ensure that the next viral movement is rooted in truth, empathy, and understanding—qualities that are vital in addressing the complexities of our modern world. The algorithms that shape our digital experiences may be intricate, but our commitment to fostering an inclusive and informed public conversation can lead us toward a more enlightened society.

In an age where ideas can spread like wildfire, we hold the power to shape the stories that define our culture. By understanding the dynamics of the digital landscape, we can actively participate in a dialogue that drives positive change. As we use digital platforms to amplify our voices and connect with others, we must wield this power thoughtfully, nurturing a conversation that reflects the diversity and richness of human experience. Every click, share, and comment has the potential to sway the conversation, and in this interconnected world, we each have a role in shaping our collective narrative.

Chapter 5: Super-Spreaders and Influencers

Profiles of Super-Spreaders

Some people have a unique ability to share ideas that can change the way we think and live. These super-spreaders, often called influencers, are more than just popular figures; they actively shape the stories that influence our beliefs, actions, and cultural values. To truly understand who they are, we need to look beyond their fame. We must explore their backgrounds, the causes they support, and how they effectively share their messages with the world.

Take Malala Yousafzai, for example. Her name has become a symbol for the fight for global education. Growing up in a small town in Pakistan, Malala's journey to the United Nations shows just how powerful personal stories can be in changing public opinion. After she survived a brutal attack by the Taliban at just 15 years old for standing up for girls' education, her story struck a chord around the world. It broke through cultural differences and sparked a movement for educational equity. For Malala, her activism is about more than just promoting education; it highlights the severe consequences of denying this basic right. Her journey is a testament to the struggles and victories that come with fighting for a cause that resonates with all of humanity. Through social media, she connects with her followers, who not only share her content but also tell their own stories, creating a collective narrative that strengthens her mission.

Another fascinating figure is Elon Musk, a giant in the world of innovation. His influence reaches far beyond technology and touches on important topics like environmental sustainability and space exploration. Companies like Tesla and SpaceX represent more than just business ventures; they embody a vision for a future that inspires millions. Musk is an intriguing mix of boldness and honesty, often sharing both his successes and failures on Twitter. This openness creates a connection with his audience, making them feel like they are part of his exciting journey. When he tweets about ambitious goals like colonizing Mars or achieving sustainable energy, he doesn't just generate buzz; he ignites a movement that encourages others to dream big and envision a better future.

In the world of social justice, Greta Thunberg stands out as a powerful voice for a generation that is frustrated yet determined. The Swedish activist's straightforward, no-nonsense approach to climate change has struck a chord with millions, especially young people who feel let down by traditional political systems. Thunberg's Fridays for Future movement began as a lone protest outside the Swedish parliament and quickly grew into a global phenomenon, showcasing the strength of grassroots activism. She has an incredible gift for explaining complex environmental issues in a way that everyone can understand, allowing her to connect with a broad audience. Whether she's addressing world leaders at the United Nations or chatting with followers on social media, her message is clear: we need to take urgent action against climate change, not just because we want to, but because it's the right thing to do.

Looking at these super-spreaders, we notice some common traits that unite them: authenticity, relatability, and clarity in their messages. Authenticity plays a key role in their influence. Each of these individuals has a personal connection to their causes, whether through their own experiences or deep passion, which builds trust with their followers. They also know how to communicate in ways that resonate with the everyday struggles and hopes of their audiences, making their messages feel reachable and actionable.

We can't overlook the importance of digital platforms, either. Social media gives these influencers the tools to quickly spread their ideas far and wide. They use the algorithms of platforms like Instagram, Twitter, and TikTok to share their thoughts and build communities around shared values and goals. Engaging directly with followers builds a sense of belonging and encourages people to become active supporters of the causes they care about.

The diversity of these super-spreaders is also striking. They operate in various fields, from technology and activism to education and entertainment. Each area presents different challenges and opportunities for influence. For example, Kim Kardashian uses her celebrity to advocate for criminal justice reform, showing how those in the entertainment industry can drive change. Her #FreeTheSlaves initiative raises awareness about mass incarceration and the unfairness in the legal system. This illustrates that super-spreaders aren't limited to a single narrative; they can fluidly navigate multiple areas of influence.

As we ponder how ideas spread, we see that these super-spreaders play crucial roles. They are not just conveyors of information; they are sparks for change, pushing us to rethink what we believe and how we act. Their ability to gather support and ignite passion highlights the significant impact one person can have in our interconnected world.

However, it's also important to consider the ethical side of their influence. With great power comes great responsibility. Super-spreaders hold a lot of sway over public opinion, and the ideas they promote can either inspire meaningful movements or spread misinformation. Their role goes beyond merely sharing ideas; they have a duty to ensure that what they promote is truthful and sincere.

The phenomenon of super-spreaders encourages us to reflect on the influential figures in our own lives. Who amplifies our beliefs? Which ideas do we feel compelled to support because of their influence? By understanding the profiles of these super-spreaders, we not only deepen our understanding of how ideas spread but also encourage ourselves to engage thoughtfully with the voices that shape our world.

In a time when information is everywhere but often confusing, super-spreaders shine like beacons. Their unique journeys show us how ideas can break barriers and inspire change. As we navigate this complex landscape of beliefs, we should stay alert and develop the ability to recognize which ideas are worth supporting and which might lead us in the wrong direction. The stories of these influential figures remind us that while ideas can spread like wildfire, the integrity behind them is what truly defines their impact on society.

Mechanisms of Influence

To truly grasp how super-spreaders amplify their ideas and inspire change on a large scale, we need to take a close look at the key elements that drive their influence. These factors work together in a fascinating way, combining charisma, credibility, smart use of platforms, and strong network connections. Each piece plays a role in giving these individuals the power to shape opinions and practices, allowing them to rise above mere popularity and become real cultural icons.

Charisma is a huge part of influence. It's that special quality that draws people in and makes them want to listen. Figures like Malala, Elon Musk, and Greta Thunberg have a magnetic presence that captivates audiences, and it's not just luck. Charisma can be developed through effective communication skills—both spoken and unspoken. The way they share their messages, often using storytelling to touch on emotions, is what makes them so appealing.

Think about storytelling for a moment: it's been a basic way of sharing experiences since humans first communicated. When influencers tell their stories, they create deep emotional connections with their audience. For example, Malala's journey isn't just about advocating for education; it's a powerful story of resilience and bravery. By sharing her experiences, she turns big ideas into relatable human stories that resonate strongly with her followers. This emotional connection is vital, as it helps people feel a sense of belonging and purpose, motivating them to support the cause.

Beyond the words they say, the non-verbal cues of super-spreaders—like body language, tone, and facial expressions—add another layer to their messages. When Greta

Thunberg stands in front of world leaders, her earnest look and strong posture communicate the urgency of her message. These non-verbal signals reinforce the sincerity of their passion, encouraging others to join them on their journeys. It's like they're not just speaking; they're inviting everyone to share in their mission, making each follower feel like a vital part of a larger movement.

In addition to charisma, perceived credibility and authority play a big role in an influencer's ability to sway public opinion. Trust is key to whether people are willing to embrace the ideas being put forward. Super-spreaders often build their reputations by showing expertise in their areas. Take Elon Musk, for example. He's not just an entrepreneur but a visionary whose work in technology and energy gives weight to his ideas about the future. His projects—from electric cars to space travel—are backed by years of experience and success; this credibility allows him to push for groundbreaking ideas with confidence.

In the digital age, authority can also be boosted through credentials and recognition. Influencers often highlight their achievements, whether through awards, collaborations, or endorsements. This collection of accolades helps create an image of expertise that audiences are more likely to believe in. Malala's journey began with a single protest, but her consistent message and the support of scientific communities have solidified her status as a trustworthy voice in the climate movement.

Building trust isn't just about past successes; it also involves ongoing engagement and honesty. Malala, for instance, stays deeply linked to her cause, frequently sharing updates and championing educational rights. This ongoing conversation establishes a bond of trust with her followers, who start to see her not just as a leader but as a fellow traveler working towards a shared goal. In this way, trust becomes a valuable currency that super-spreaders invest in, repaying them over time as they continue to connect genuinely with their audience.

The platforms influencers choose to use also play a crucial role in expanding their reach. The rise of digital media has made communication accessible to everyone, letting ideas spread quickly across various channels. Social media sites like Twitter, Instagram, and TikTok are now vital tools for influencers. These platforms create opportunities for direct interaction with a global audience, allowing followers to engage, share, and boost messages instantly.

For instance, Elon Musk's activity on Twitter showcases how one person can influence conversations and rally support through concise, impactful posts. His tweets often ignite discussions and set social media trends, demonstrating the power of a well-timed message. This clever use of social media can turn a simple thought into a viral sensation, showing how the medium can enhance the message.

However, it's not just about being on social media; it's about recognizing the unique qualities of each platform. Different platforms attract different crowds, and smart influencers tailor their content to fit those audiences. Greta Thunberg, for example, uses Instagram to communicate not only her message but also to connect with younger people who often prefer visual media. Her posts blend eye-catching images with strong, concise text, sparking engagement and motivating followers to share her content widely.

Super-spreaders also know how to use traditional media alongside digital platforms. The power of public speaking shouldn't be overlooked; speeches at conferences, interviews on TV, and participation in discussions all help influencers reach a broader audience. By mixing these methods, they create a well-rounded approach to influence that spreads their ideas across different channels, ensuring they connect with as many people as possible.

Still, the ways of influence aren't just about individual action; they are also shaped by the networks super-spreaders work within. Social capital—the relationships and connections one has in their community—greatly enhances the ability to share ideas. Influencers often connect with others, partnering with peers to amplify their messages and gain momentum.

Take Malala's collaborations with other activists and organizations as an example. By joining forces with fellow advocates for educational rights, she not only increases her reach but also enriches her message with different perspectives. Each collaborator adds their own voice to the mix, creating a powerful wave of advocacy that resonates strongly with audiences. This network effect shows how ideas can gain power when supported by a collective effort rather than just one person.

The influence of peer networks is also significant. When people see their friends, family, or admired figures supporting a cause, they are more likely to adopt those beliefs themselves. This idea is rooted in social psychology; individuals tend to align their opinions with those they feel are part of their community. By strategically placing themselves within influential circles, super-spreaders can boost their ideas through social proof, motivating others to join in simply because it seems popular or accepted.

Moreover, the dynamics of these networks can be affected by the echo chamber effect. Social media algorithms often filter content to match users' existing beliefs, creating an environment where ideas can thrive without opposition. This situation has its pros and cons. On one hand, it helps influencers engage deeply with their loyal followers; on the other, it can lead to the spread of misinformation if differing views are silenced. Super-spreaders need to be cautious since their influence goes beyond just the messages they promote; it also includes their impact on the overall discussion within their networks.

By examining these mechanisms, we can gain insights into why some super-spreaders are more successful at mobilizing ideas than others. It's not just about having charisma or a powerful platform; it's the intricate combination of communication, credibility, and network dynamics that fuels their influence. To replicate these successful strategies, authenticity and real connections with the audience are key. Anyone looking to make a difference should embrace these qualities while sharpening their storytelling skills and understanding the platforms available to them.

Ultimately, the ways of influence remind us that ideas don't thrive on their own. They flourish within a rich ecosystem of relationships, stories, and social structures. As we navigate the changing landscape of beliefs and advocacy, the lessons from today's super-spreaders highlight the significant role that effective communication and strategic engagement play in shaping our shared understanding. As we reflect on our own contributions in this dynamic environment, we should aim to embody the traits that make these influencers so impactful, creating connections that empower us to engage in the important work of fostering understanding and driving meaningful change.

Impact on Public Opinion

In a world where information flies around at lightning speed, super-spreaders hold a special power that goes beyond just being popular. These individuals have a remarkable ability to shape the conversations we have, influencing how society thinks about important issues. The discussions they spark can lead to movements, inspire social change, and even sway public policy. When these influencers share their thoughts online, they create ripples that touch the lives and beliefs of millions. This chapter looks closely at the significant impact these influential figures have on public opinion, exploring how they reach people and the ethical responsibilities that come with their influence.

Every chat we have is influenced by the stories pushed by public figures. How they present new ideas or change the way we view existing ones can lead to real change—sometimes in small ways, other times in major ways, but always in ways that matter. Take the Black Lives Matter movement, for instance. It gained traction partly because super-spreaders on social media shared powerful messages about systemic racism, police violence, and social justice. The hashtag #BlackLivesMatter became a powerful call to action, uniting people and inspiring real-life change.

A turning point happened in 2020 when protests erupted around the globe after George Floyd was killed. Influencers from all walks of life—celebrities, politicians, and activists—used their platforms to show their support. Their involvement brought attention to the movement, pushing it into mainstream conversations. This flood of voices not only highlighted the urgency of the issues at hand but also shifted how the public viewed police reform and racial justice. It demonstrated how these super-spreaders can rally support and transform societal narratives.

However, the way public discourse evolves isn't always straightforward. Influencers often find themselves in a complicated world, carefully crafting their messages to connect with different audiences. Their skill in tailoring content to fit the preferences of various groups is key to how their ideas are received. The words they choose, the stories they share, and the emotions they stir up can really affect how well their messages hit home. For example, Greta Thunberg's approach to climate change speaks deeply to younger audiences. She mixes urgency with a relatable style, encouraging engagement. Her speeches often blend personal stories with hard facts, creating a compelling narrative that makes the looming threat of climate change feel real and urgent.

As ideas shift from being overlooked to widely accepted, super-spreaders play a vital role in this journey. They can turn once fringe concepts into mainstream beliefs, as we've seen in discussions around wellness, mental health, and social justice. Each of these topics has experienced a remarkable transformation in public conversations, moving from niche discussions to crucial dialogues that touch many parts of society. This journey usually follows a clear path: starting out obscure, gaining passionate followers, being amplified by influential figures, and eventually being embraced by the general public.

Let's look at mental health as an example. It used to be shrouded in stigma and misunderstanding, but conversations about it have changed dramatically. Influential figures like Dwayne "The Rock" Johnson and mental health advocate Brené Brown have been instrumental in normalizing discussions around mental wellness. By sharing their own stories, these super-spreaders have helped shift mental health from a taboo topic to one that is openly talked about and accepted. Their openness has encouraged countless individuals to seek help and engage in conversations that challenge long-standing societal views.

While the journey of spreading ideas can be uplifting, it also reveals potential pitfalls in the ideological landscapes that emerge from it. Normalizing certain ideas can lead to changes in cultural standards and policies. For instance, public discussions surrounding LGBTQ+ rights have transformed significantly over the last few decades, largely driven by super-spreaders and advocates who have tirelessly pushed for acceptance and equality. When public figures come out and share their experiences, they create visibility and representation, allowing society to confront biases and reshape its collective narrative.

This evolution in public attitudes is complex. The influence of super-spreaders can sometimes oversimplify intricate issues or spread misinformation. The rise of health influencers on social media has brought attention to numerous wellness trends, but it's also led to the dissemination of unverified claims and potentially harmful advice. Because super-spreaders often have large followings, their endorsements can unknowingly give credibility to incorrect or misleading information, muddying the waters of public discourse.

Ethical concerns are crucial in this landscape. With great influence comes great responsibility. Those in influential positions face moral dilemmas that come along with their reach. When super-spreaders choose to amplify certain messages, they need to think about how their narratives affect society as a whole. There's always the risk of manipulation and the danger of creating echo chambers that reinforce existing beliefs while silencing alternative views. This responsibility becomes even more significant when discussing divisive topics like politics or social justice, where the consequences of misinformation can be harmful.

Consider the impact of influencers during the COVID-19 pandemic. They have significantly affected public attitudes around vaccinations, mask-wearing, and health guidelines. While many have effectively shared accurate information, some have unfortunately fueled vaccine hesitancy and spread misinformation. The responsibility that super-spreaders have to vet the information they share extends beyond their personal narratives; it reaches into how they shape public understanding of crucial health matters. A single tweet or post can set off a chain reaction, highlighting the need for discernment and accountability among those with significant influence.

As we think about the broader effects of super-spreaders on public opinion, it becomes clear that their role is both transformative and filled with challenges. They can drive positive change, shining a light on vital issues and altering societal norms. Yet, they also bear the weight of ethical responsibility, as their influence can lead to unintended consequences that flow through the ideological landscape. The impact of super-spreaders goes beyond individual stories; it's a collective phenomenon that requires careful thought from both influencers and their audiences.

The connection between super-spreaders and the public is a two-way street. While influencers can shape opinions, they are also shaped by the feelings of their followers. This back-and-forth relationship shows how important it is to engage critically with the content we consume and share. As active participants in this exchange of ideas, we need to be aware of our roles in the ideological marketplace, recognizing that our involvement helps shape the narratives that dominate public conversations.

Ultimately, the phenomenon of super-spreaders reflects our interconnected world, where ideas can spread rapidly, sparking movements and challenging deeply held beliefs. The influence of these figures reminds us of the power of communication and the responsibility that comes with it. As we navigate the complexities of modern society, we should engage thoughtfully with the stories shaping our beliefs and practices. In doing so, we can create an environment where ideas are not just circulated but examined, challenged, and transformed into something that aligns with our collective dreams for a fairer and more just world.

Chapter 6: Crises as Catalysts

Crises: The Breeding Ground for Change

Crises often serve as the spark that ignites a fire within a society, shaking things up in ways that can be both subtle and dramatic. These chaotic moments—whether they arise from economic downturns, political upheavals, social protests, or environmental disasters—force us to take a hard look at the world around us. They challenge the way things have always been and push individuals and groups to reconsider their beliefs and values. It's truly fascinating to see how one single event can echo throughout society, leaving a trail of changed perspectives in its wake.

Consider the global financial crisis of 2008. This disaster didn't just ruin lives; it also made people rethink capitalism itself. The fallout led to movements like Occupy Wall Street, which shone a spotlight on the gap between the rich and the poor, bringing discussions about economic inequality into everyday conversation. This crisis, like many before it, revealed a huge divide between what was widely accepted and the actual experiences of so many people. When the traditional systems fail to offer solutions, it opens the door for fresh ideas to take root, allowing voices that were once silenced to emerge and demand change.

Crises create an environment ripe for new ideas by breaking down the mental barriers that keep people stuck in old beliefs. During uncertain times, fear and anxiety can spark a collective rethinking of our values and priorities. People who once accepted the status quo might start to question long-held beliefs, looking for alternatives that not only offer hope but also a sense of control in a chaotic world. This is especially true with the rise of populist movements, where charismatic leaders tap into the frustrations arising from crises to gather support for bold changes. They often present themselves as the champions of the everyday person, framing their ideas as the solution to the problems caused by the elite or the establishment.

The psychological impact of collective behavior during crises is significant. Humans are social beings, and when faced with turmoil, they instinctively come together—sometimes in constructive ways, other times not so much. During these turbulent times, mass mobilization often thrives. People gather, protests erupt, and communities unite around shared grievances. This powerful collective energy can quickly spread new ideas, turning individuals into advocates for change. The sheer force of people coming together can bring forward ideologies that might have stayed hidden or marginalized when times were more stable.

A perfect illustration of this is the Arab Spring. In 2010, a fruit vendor in Tunisia set himself on fire in protest against police corruption and mistreatment, triggering a wave of protests across the Middle East and North Africa. What started as a local issue rapidly transformed into a broader movement against authoritarian regimes, with citizens demanding democracy, social justice, and economic opportunities. Social media became a crucial tool in this ideological shift, allowing information to spread quickly and helping people mobilize for protests, echoing feelings that had been simmering for a long time.

While it's easy to be optimistic about how crises can lead to positive change, it's also important to recognize that this process can have both positive and negative outcomes. The same conditions that inspire forward-thinking movements can also give rise to harmful ideologies. History is full of examples where crises have propelled extremist beliefs into the spotlight. After World War I, for instance, Germany saw the rise of the Nazi Party. Economic instability and national humiliation created a breeding ground for xenophobia and authoritarianism. This serves as a sobering reminder that crises can lead societies either toward enlightenment or into darkness.

As we navigate the complex aftermath of crises, it's vital to consider the historical context that shapes the ideologies that emerge. Every crisis carries the weight of past grievances, cultural stories, and societal structures. For instance, the Great Depression led to the rise of Keynesian economics as policymakers sought solutions to a failing capitalist system. This ideological shift during that time significantly changed the role of government in the economy, impacting American capitalism for decades.

The relationship between crisis and ideology isn't just about large historical events; even smaller personal crises can lead to significant changes within individuals. Take someone facing an unexpected health diagnosis, for instance. Such life-altering moments can trigger a deep reevaluation of what truly matters, prompting individuals to adopt new philosophies or lifestyles they might have overlooked before. In this way, crises can spark personal growth and ideological shifts on both small and large scales.

To understand how crises shape belief systems, we can look at key historical moments that have reshaped our views. From the American Civil Rights Movement to the feminist movements that began in the 1960s and beyond, these pivotal events show how crises can inspire action and create new frameworks of thought. The Civil Rights Movement, for example, was not just a reaction to racial injustice; it represented a powerful shift in ideology that challenged deeply ingrained concepts of race, equality, and justice, fundamentally changing the social landscape of America.

During times of crisis, activists often adopt new strategies and tactics that reflect the urgency of their circumstances. The rise of civil disobedience as a form of protest, popularized by leaders like Martin Luther King Jr., illustrates this evolution in the fight for justice. This approach emerged as a direct response to the violence faced by civil rights advocates, demonstrating how crises can lead to new paths in the quest for social change.

The environmental crises we face today further underline the connection between turmoil and ideology. The growing impacts of climate change have sparked a global push for sustainability and environmental justice, giving rise to ideas centered around eco-socialism and initiatives like the Green New Deal. As we experience more catastrophic events—like wildfires and hurricanes—public sentiment shifts; people start to see how interconnected we all are and the urgency of tackling climate-related challenges. This creates fertile ground for transformative ideas that challenge existing patterns of consumption and exploitation.

The ideological shifts that come from crises also highlight how technology amplifies voices and ideas. The digital age has completely changed how we communicate and advocate for change. Social media platforms allow for the quick sharing of information, making it easy for ideas to spread rapidly. This technological shift has opened up access to platforms for marginalized groups, giving them a chance to share their experiences and push for change. Recent movements for racial and social justice, often ignited by crises, have effectively used technology to organize and raise awareness, showing the close relationship between crisis, ideology, and technology.

Recognizing the role of crises as catalysts for ideological change encourages us to reflect on how we respond to the challenges we face. Instead of avoiding turbulent moments, we have the chance to engage with the ideas that arise from them. By promoting a culture of openness and curiosity, we can navigate the complexities of these ideological shifts, embracing the potential for growth and change.

In the end, crises remind us that ideologies aren't set in stone; they can grow and change. As individuals and societies confront the challenges that come with upheaval, they find themselves at a crossroads—a moment where transformation is possible. The real question isn't if crises will happen, but how we will respond and which ideas we will nurture in the fertile ground they create. In this ever-shifting landscape, the opportunity for new ideas and transformative movements is as compelling as ever, urging us to stay vigilant, open-minded, and engaged as we navigate the complexities of our shared existence.

Collective Behavior in Uncertain Times

When society faces upheaval, the reactions often carve new paths in history. Collective behavior during tough times uncovers the instincts and motivations that prompt groups to come together. Fear, uncertainty, and the desire for connection can create a powerful mix, leading to beliefs taking shape in ways that might never happen in calmer times. It's intriguing to see how individuals can respond to chaos: some may hold tighter to their beliefs, while others might open up to bold new ideas. Grasping this psychological dance is key to understanding the modern movements that spring up in response to crises.

Take the Arab Spring as a shining example of collective behavior during chaotic times. It wasn't just a wave of protests; it was a burst of shared awareness, a collective understanding that change was not only needed but possible. The spark ignited by that one Tunisian vendor, Mohamed Bouazizi, echoed throughout the region. His desperate act struck a chord with the frustrations of countless individuals. As people came together, their various complaints merged into a strong demand for democracy, social justice, and economic opportunity. This movement shows how uncertainty can rally communities, transforming passive dissatisfaction into active resistance.

At the core of this phenomenon is social identity theory, which suggests that our sense of self is greatly influenced by the groups we belong to. During crises, if people feel their group identities are under threat, they are more likely to come together to defend those identities. During the Arab Spring, a renewed sense of national identity and shared purpose fueled the protests. People stopped seeing themselves as isolated individuals; they became part of a larger story. They were not just fighting for their own sake but for their communities, their countries, and their shared identities. This collective identity can serve as a powerful motivator, pulling individuals into a common struggle for change.

However, collective behavior has its downsides too. The phenomenon of groupthink can emerge, where the desire for harmony within a group leads to poor or irrational decision-making. In the rush to unite, differing opinions may get silenced, allowing only a narrow range of beliefs to gain traction. This can create an echo chamber, where some ideas are reinforced while others are pushed aside. Such dynamics can be particularly risky during crises, where the stakes are high and the need for effective action is critical. Historical examples, like the rise of totalitarian regimes in chaotic times, remind us how groupthink can lead to disastrous choices.

Fear plays a complicated role in shaping collective behavior. It can inspire action and resistance, but it can also lead to conformity and submission. For instance, after the September 11 attacks in the United States, the fear of terrorism spurred a wave of patriotism, but it also brought about restrictions on civil liberties and the acceptance of surveillance measures that many might have previously opposed. In such moments, the collective response is a mix of emotions, where fear can push people to accept ideas that may not truly reflect their values.

As crises unfold, social networks and digital communication become crucial. The rise of social media has changed how collective action is organized. During the Arab Spring, social media wasn't just a communication tool; it became the heartbeat of the movement. Hashtags became rallying cries, and protest videos went viral, attracting international attention and support. The decentralized nature of these platforms allowed revolutionary ideas and strategies to spread quickly. For many activists, social media offered a break from state-controlled narratives, allowing them to share their stories and rally others in real-time.

Yet, this digital landscape brings up important questions about the authenticity of collective actions. Information spreads easily, making it just as easy for misinformation to flourish. Viral trends can ignite movements, but they can also create confusion and division. The challenge is figuring out which ideas are worth supporting and which might lead to further discord. This reliance on digital communication underscores the need for careful engagement with the sources and messages being shared.

Moral shocks are also key to understanding how crises can spark collective action. Moral shocks are unexpected events that trigger strong emotional reactions, prompting individuals to act in ways they might not have otherwise considered. The Black Lives Matter movement gained traction after the tragic death of George Floyd, with the shocking footage of his killing sparking a moral outcry. This emotional response rippled around the world, leading to protests and renewed discussions about systemic racism. Such crises can push people to rethink their beliefs and get involved in activism.

These moral shocks often expose the deep contradictions in society. They highlight injustices that might have gone unnoticed or ignored. When people see or experience these shocks, they often feel compelled to fight for justice or change. This is where activism and group mobilization thrive. Crises not only provide a backdrop for collective behavior but also create the conditions necessary for movements to rise and persist.

The stories of various social movements throughout history show how crises can drive activism and ideological shifts. Think of the feminist movements of the 1960s; the societal upheaval from civil rights struggles, anti-war protests, and economic changes encouraged many women to challenge their roles. The collective behavior of women, connected by shared experiences and grievances, led to significant social changes and a rethinking of gender norms. The unity forged during crises allowed for a new dialogue about gender equality that continues to this day.

Environmental movements have also tapped into crises to spark collective action. As awareness of climate change grows, initiatives focused on sustainability and environmental justice have gained momentum. Activists have harnessed moral shocks—like severe weather events or the extinction of species—to rally public support and inspire action. The pressing nature of these crises pushes individuals to face uncomfortable truths about consumption and its effects on the planet. In this way, crises not only act as catalysts for change but also create opportunities for new ways of thinking about sustainability and our connections to one another.

Technology plays a vital role in this context. The internet and social media have reshaped how movements are organized and how ideas are shared. Activists can now tell their stories and share strategies across the globe in real-time, making activism more accessible. This democratization allows voices from marginalized communities to be heard in ways that were previously impossible. The interconnectedness that technology provides empowers individuals to engage with global movements and issues, fostering a sense of solidarity that crosses borders.

Despite the potential for positive change, the landscape of collective behavior during crises is full of challenges. The risks of fragmentation, misinformation, and extremist ideologies are ever-present. Movements must navigate these complexities while trying to hold onto their core values and goals. The mix of thoughts within movements can be both a strength and a weakness; it encourages innovation and flexibility but can also lead to internal conflict and disagreement.

Ultimately, exploring collective behavior during uncertain times uncovers a rich blend of motivations, emotions, and beliefs. By understanding how fear, social identity, and moral shocks shape group responses, we can better appreciate the nuances of social movements. As crises continue to arise in various forms, the ability to unite and take collective action will remain a vital part of societal change. By recognizing the potential for transformation in crises, we can harness the power of collective behavior to tackle the pressing issues of our time and work towards a fairer and more just future. In a world filled with uncertainty, the ability of our ideas to adapt and evolve reminds us of the resilience of the human spirit and our ongoing pursuit of progress.

Historical Turning Points

History isn't just a timeline of events; it's a rich blend of ideas, beliefs, and actions that shape our societies. While political changes, economic struggles, and social movements ebb and flow, there are moments that stand out as true turning points. These pivotal events do more than leave an immediate impact; they mark significant changes in how people see themselves and their role in the world.

One of the most memorable moments is the fall of the Berlin Wall in 1989. This wasn't just about tearing down a structure; it symbolized the end of an ideology that had split Europe for decades. For many years, the wall represented the Cold War and the fierce battle between capitalism and communism. When it fell, it was a powerful message: the people of East Germany, along with many in Eastern Europe, were no longer willing to accept the oppressive governments that constrained their lives. The joyful scenes of people climbing over the wall, chipping away at its concrete, and celebrating their new freedom were not just acts of happiness; they were a united stand against an ideology that had suppressed personal and cultural expression.

Leading up to this moment, the socio-political scene was ready for change. Throughout the 1980s, reform-minded leaders began to rise in Eastern Europe, inspired by the ideas of Soviet leader Mikhail Gorbachev, especially his policies of glasnost (openness) and perestroika (restructuring). These policies inspired many dissidents and everyday citizens to dream of a brighter future—one filled with democracy, freedom of speech, and the right to gather without fear. The fall of the Berlin Wall represented the peak of these aspirations, signaling the end of one era and the dawn of a new ideological time in Europe.

But the impact of this turning point extended well beyond Germany's borders. It sent shockwaves around the globe, fueling movements and political changes in places like the Soviet Union, where the legitimacy of communism began to falter as republics sought independence. It also reignited conversations about freedom and democracy worldwide, proving that when one oppressive regime falls, it can inspire others to rise up against their own governments. This shift in ideology, born from the Berlin Wall's collapse, opened the doors for democratic movements everywhere, demonstrating that united action can bring about significant change.

Another moment that reshaped global politics was the September 11 attacks in 2001. The tragedy that unfolded that day claimed thousands of lives and triggered a massive shift in beliefs, especially in the United States. In the beginning, there was an overwhelming sense of shock and sorrow. But soon, this transformed into a wave of nationalism, a drive for justice, and a heightened awareness of vulnerability. The attacks changed how people talked about security, civil liberties, and foreign relations.

In the aftermath of 9/11, a very real fear swept through the nation. The idea of American exceptionalism changed, creating a clear divide between "us" and "them." What once celebrated freedom and democracy was now viewed through the lens of safety and protection. New policies, such as the controversial Patriot Act, were put in place, expanding government surveillance and limiting civil liberties in the name of national security. Conversations about terrorism began to dominate political discussions, resulting in military actions in Afghanistan and Iraq that would have lasting effects on international relations.

What's intriguing about these shifts in ideology is how they reveal the ongoing cycle of crises and the reactions they provoke. In response to the attacks, the U.S. government's actions were not just about revenge; they tapped into deeper fears and insecurities that already existed. The narrative of a nation under threat sparked a wave of patriotism, with people rallying around their leaders and the government. But this also led to division and dissent, as movements advocating for civil liberties, like the ACLU's campaigns against government spying, emerged as a counter to the dominant narrative of fear and security.

Fast forward to a more recent turning point: the COVID-19 pandemic. The arrival of the coronavirus in early 2020 created an unprecedented crisis that touched every part of the globe, changing how we interact, work, and connect with each other. The pandemic not only exposed weaknesses in public health systems but also laid bare long-standing inequalities in society. The ideological effects of COVID-19 have been wide-ranging, sparking a reconsideration of social norms, work-life balance, and the government's role in health care.

As communities faced lockdowns and restrictions, the pandemic inspired a wave of collective action reminiscent of past crises. People banded together through mutual aid networks, reaching out to neighbors and local groups to lend a hand. The idea of community took on a new importance as individuals recognized how vital social connections are in uncertain times. The dominant belief in individualism in many Western cultures was challenged as people saw the need for mutual support to overcome shared struggles.

COVID-19 also reshaped the conversation around health care and social safety nets. As the virus hit hard, public health became a hot topic, sparking debates about access to medical care, government responsibilities, and corporate roles in health. Movements advocating for universal health care gained momentum, driven by the stark realities revealed by the pandemic. The ideological landscape shifted as people began to question whether current systems were adequate and explored alternatives that focused on public well-being over profits.

Additionally, the pandemic highlighted the systemic inequalities that had long been overlooked. The disproportionate impact on marginalized communities, particularly people of color and low-income individuals, became a focal point for social justice movements. The rise of Black Lives Matter protests during this time underscored how interconnected these crises are—health disparities, racial injustice, and economic inequality. The shift from viewing these issues as separate to recognizing their connections has renewed calls for comprehensive reform.

Reflecting on these historical turning points reveals that crises can be powerful catalysts for change, reshaping and reshuffling belief systems. Each event—the fall of the Berlin Wall, the September 11 attacks, and the COVID-19 pandemic—has acted like a mirror, showing us the prevailing ideologies while also raising new questions and discussions.

What stands out is how these moments have not just led to quick changes but have also created lasting effects on public conversations and policies. The lessons learned from these pivotal events, especially about the importance of collective action and thoughtful engagement with ideologies, are crucial as we navigate today's challenges.

Crises reveal how fragile our beliefs can be, and they can inspire bold reimaginations of society. They remind us that ideologies aren't fixed; they grow and change based on the world we live in. Just as the fall of the Berlin Wall marked the end of one era, moments of crisis encourage us to rethink our values, question the status quo, and dream of a future that emphasizes equity, justice, and the well-being of all.

The ongoing cycle of crises and ideological shifts shows us that history isn't just a series of disconnected events but a continuous flow of struggles and victories. As we face current and future challenges, the insights gained from past turning points remind us that crises can be opportunities for reinvention. They push us to question, to unite, and to envision a better future, highlighting that the beliefs we hold can shape not just our societies but also what it means to be human.

Ultimately, while crises may bring chaos and uncertainty, they also hold the promise of major transformation. They challenge us to reconsider our beliefs, to stand together in tough times, and to navigate the ideological landscape with open minds. As we move forward, let's remember that each turning point is not just an end but a chance to imagine a more just and equitable world. In the face of crises, we have the strength to respond with resilience and creativity, forging new paths in our shared journey toward a brighter future.

Chapter 7: Evolution and Mutation of Ideas

Memetic Evolution

Picture a world where ideas are not just passing thoughts, but lively beings that thrive in a cultural garden. In this colorful landscape, ideas, much like living organisms, undergo their own form of growth and change. This fascinating idea is wrapped up in the concept of memes, which are the building blocks of cultural exchange. Coined by evolutionary biologist Richard Dawkins in his 1976 book, "The Selfish Gene," the term "meme" refers to any piece of information that can spread and multiply within a culture. Just like genes that pass on biological traits, memes carry cultural traits, moving through groups of people and adjusting to their surroundings.

At the core of this process of memetic evolution are three key concepts: variation, selection, and retention. These ideas echo the principles of Darwinian evolution, suggesting that thoughts and beliefs also have to navigate the ups and downs of survival in a changing world. Let's take a closer look at each of these concepts to see how they play out in the spread of ideas throughout history and in today's society.

Variation is the first important step in the journey of ideas. Just as genetic mutations create diversity among living things, ideas can also change as they travel from one person or culture to another. This isn't just a minor detail; it's crucial for the survival of ideas in a world that is always shifting. When ideas are shared, they can be influenced by the places they are expressed, the beliefs of those sharing them, and the cultures that receive them. For instance, consider political ideas like democracy or socialism—the changes they undergo can be surprisingly significant.

Take democracy, for instance. The original idea of democracy in ancient Athens looks very different from the democratic systems we know today. Back then, only a small group of people—free male citizens—had a say in government. As time went on and society changed, the idea of democracy evolved as well. It began to allow more people to take part, leading to universal voting rights in many countries. This change is a direct response to the needs and challenges of society, showing how ideas can shift to stay relevant.

Socialism has also seen major changes since it emerged in the 19th century. Karl Marx's vision of socialism included a classless society where everyone shared ownership of production. However, as societies worked to implement such a radical shift, different versions popped up—like democratic socialism, which seeks to mix political democracy with social ownership. This ability to change is essential for ideas to survive and thrive, reminding us that they aren't fixed but instead can adapt to the flow of cultural evolution.

Next up is the selection process in memetic evolution, which is all about how certain ideas rise to the top while others fade away. This selection is influenced by a mix of psychological, social, and technological factors. For instance, cognitive biases significantly impact how we receive and share ideas. People naturally tend to favor information that matches their existing beliefs, a phenomenon called confirmation bias. This means that ideas that resonate with our emotions and thoughts are more likely to spread.

Social dynamics also play a big role in which ideas take off. Groupthink can cause communities to rally around specific beliefs, stifling dissent and alternative viewpoints.

When people in a group share a strong identity, they often prioritize unity over questioning ideas. This can lead to dominant narratives that overshadow other voices, influencing which concepts flourish and which ones fade away.

Moreover, technology—especially social media algorithms—has become increasingly important in determining which ideas gain traction. These algorithms curate content based on what users prefer and how they behave, often leading to echo chambers where similar ideas are amplified while differing opinions are drowned out. Picture scrolling through your social media feed filled with memes and articles that reinforce a specific ideology—this careful selection of information can greatly affect how ideas spread. As algorithms prioritize engagement, sensational ideas often get more attention, even if they are not backed by facts.

The final piece of memetic evolution is retention, which is all about how certain ideas stick around in our societal values and norms. While variation and selection are vital for spreading ideas, retention is what allows them to become ingrained over time. Some ideas manage to weave themselves into the fabric of society, becoming widely accepted and resistant to change. A great example of this is the growing acceptance of sustainability in business.

In recent years, concepts like corporate social responsibility and environmental sustainability have moved from the sidelines to the forefront of business practices. This shift has been driven by various factors, such as consumer demand, regulatory changes, and increased global awareness of environmental issues. As companies start to see the importance of sustainable practices, these ideas have gained ground and become part of corporate culture.

Consider the rise of the term "greenwashing," which describes when companies mislead consumers about the environmental benefits of their products or practices. This term came about as a response to the growing focus on sustainability, highlighting how critically consumers view corporate actions. The fact that such terms are now part of everyday conversation shows how certain ideas not only endure but also thrive, shaping behaviors and expectations in meaningful ways.

Looking through history, we can see many examples of memetic evolution at work. The idea of "free love," which gained traction during the sexual revolution of the 1960s, serves as a compelling case of how ideas can change over time. Initially rooted in the desire to break free from traditional views on relationships and sexuality, "free love" embraced a bold vision of connections free from societal constraints. As culture shifted and new challenges arose—like the AIDS crisis and evolving conversations about consent—the idea underwent significant transformation.

Today, discussions about free love are often intertwined with modern ideas of consent, autonomy, and inclusivity. The concept hasn't disappeared; instead, it has adapted to reflect the values and concerns of contemporary society. The journey of this idea reminds us of the fluid nature of memes, illustrating how they can evolve to align with the priorities of different generations.

By exploring the mechanisms of memetic evolution—variation, selection, and retention—we gain a better understanding of the lively nature of ideas in our world. The ongoing exchange of cultural ideas ensures that they are never stagnant; they grow, change, and thrive based on their environments. Recognizing these mechanisms deepens our appreciation for how ideas shape our individual and shared experiences, encouraging us to think about our roles as active participants in the world of ideas.

As we navigate the winding paths of ideas and their evolution, it's essential to stay alert. The memes that are popular today may not hold the same appeal tomorrow. The realm of ideas is always shifting, reminding us of the responsibility we carry in shaping the stories that make up our world. The true power of ideas lies not only in their ability to influence but also in their potential to change, push boundaries, and challenge norms as they seek relevance and meaning.

Hybridization of Concepts

When we think about ideas, hybridization is like a secret ingredient that stirs up creativity and change in our culture. Imagine a lab filled with colorful liquids in vials, where each vial symbolizes a different idea—whether it's art, technology, philosophy, or social movements. When we mix these liquids together, we often see something surprising and beautiful happen. Just like in these experiments, blending ideas can create powerful results that shake up old ways of thinking and inspire new possibilities. Hybridization is not just about smashing concepts together; it's like an intricate dance that mirrors the complexity of the world around us.

Hybridization thrives on the understanding that no idea stands alone. Every notion is shaped by those that came before it and those that are happening at the same time. This constant exchange leads to a lively process where ideas borrow from one another, forming a rich blend of thoughts that changes over time. Take "hacktivism," for example. This is where ethical hackers combine their tech skills with political activism. It shows us that technology isn't just for fun or profit; it can also be a powerful tool for social justice. Hacktivists act with strong moral beliefs, viewing the digital world as a space for significant change. Their acts, often carried out anonymously, can unveil corruption, raise awareness about pressing issues, and bring communities together. The mix of technology and activism is a trailblazing example of how hybridization can spark new movements that question and challenge established powers.

As we dig deeper into hybridization, it's clear that it often arises as a response to complex social issues. For instance, when traditional mindfulness practices are blended with modern psychological therapy, we get mindfulness-based stress reduction (MBSR). This fresh approach combines age-old techniques of meditation and awareness with contemporary therapeutic methods, providing people with effective tools to cope with stress and anxiety. MBSR has found its way into many settings, from corporate offices to schools, showing how hybrid ideas can deeply connect with today's audiences. This method not only improves mental health practices but also reflects a broader cultural shift toward holistic well-being.

However, mixing different concepts is not always straightforward. Successfully combining ideas requires a thoughtful understanding of each part involved. It calls for being open to new perspectives and a willingness to step outside the boundaries of traditional thinking. Look at how distinct musical genres blend to create entirely new sounds that resonate with many listeners. Consider the fusion of jazz and hip-hop, where spontaneous melodies meet rhythmic beats. This kind of hybridization has given rise to legendary artists and unforgettable albums that break the mold, showcasing the artistic possibilities that come from mixing cultural expressions.

Yet, hybridization isn't just confined to the arts or technology; it affects every aspect of human life. In social movements, we can see various ideologies come together to form impactful coalitions. For instance, the merging of environmentalism and social justice has led to the environmental justice movement. This blend highlights how those in marginalized communities often suffer the most from environmental harm. By joining the goals of ecological sustainability with a commitment to social equality, activists are paving the way for a fairer and more inclusive world.

The power of hybrid ideas goes well beyond just individual projects or movements. They can challenge existing norms, disrupt industries, and reshape cultural stories. When we look at how these hybrid concepts develop, we see their influence spreading across different fields, from politics to business. The rise of social entrepreneurship is a perfect example, where innovative companies aim to create social value alongside financial success. Businesses that blend profit with a mission for social change are redefining what it means to act responsibly. This hybrid approach not only tackles urgent social problems but also resonates with consumers who are increasingly focused on ethical choices.

Furthermore, the mix of science and art creates exciting opportunities for hybridization. Take bioart, for example. This form of art combines artistic creativity with biological science, challenging how we view life and nature. Artists and scientists work together to create pieces that provoke thought and spark conversations about topics like genetic engineering, biopreservation, and environmental sustainability. These hybrids act as a bridge between different fields, inviting people to engage with challenging scientific ideas while also connecting emotionally through art. In this way, hybridization deepens our connection to the ideas that shape our understanding of the world.

As we examine how hybrid ideas influence societal change, it becomes clear that they are crucial for navigating the complexities we face today. In a time of fast technological progress and shifting cultural values, hybridization paves the way for innovation. It encourages us to think beyond rigid categories and embrace the fluid nature of ideas. By adopting a mindset that prioritizes collaboration and sharing across disciplines, we can unlock new paths for growth and progress.

Looking to the future of hybridization, we must recognize the challenges that come with this blending process. As we mix ideas, we should be cautious about the risk of undermining or watering down marginalized voices. Hybridization should be approached with care, understanding the historical context and power dynamics that shape how we view various concepts. It's important to engage in thoughtful conversations and collaborations that respect the origins of ideas while promoting inclusivity and diversity.

In the end, hybridization of concepts is a testament to human creativity and the endless potential of ideas. It invites us to rethink the limits of our thinking and embrace the richness that arises when different perspectives come together. As we navigate life's complexities, we are reminded that blending ideas can lead to remarkable transformations, sparking movements that resonate deeply within our societies. In a time when we face many challenges that require innovative solutions, hybridization stands out not just as a strategy for progress, but as a celebration of the interconnectedness of our human experience.

Survival of the Fittest Ideas

Ideas, much like living things, often find themselves in a competitive arena where only the strongest and most adaptable make it through. In this lively environment of thoughts and beliefs, some concepts thrive while others fade away. The phrase "survival of the fittest," first used by Charles Darwin to explain natural selection, gives us an intriguing way to look at the changing and sometimes chaotic landscape of our cultural discussions. Just like species change to fit their surroundings, ideas must also grow and change to capture attention, stay relevant, and make an impact in a world that is always in flux.

At the core of this idea survival are the concepts of relevance and resonance. In a world overflowing with information, the ideas that connect with people tend to have a better chance of flourishing. Take, for instance, the rise of environmentalism. This movement has gained significant momentum in recent years, largely due to increased awareness of climate change and the damage to our ecosystems. It's not just the scientific facts driving this movement; it's the emotional connections that environmentalism creates—a heartfelt appeal to our desire for a better, sustainable future.

The urgency of climate issues taps into our values, encouraging people to unite and support a common cause. This shared connection fuels an idea's growth, allowing it to spread quickly through communities, social media, and local initiatives.

The mood of society plays a key role in deciding which ideas come to the forefront. When people's needs shift, the ideas that capture their attention often change as well. For example, during times of crisis, ideas that emphasize community and working together tend to gain traction. This was especially clear during the COVID-19 pandemic, where the focus on collective well-being and mutual support became vital. The phrase "we are all in this together" echoed in conversations, leading to a rise in community-focused efforts and support networks. The strength of these ideas reflects not only the challenges faced but also a deep longing for connection and solidarity during tough times.

Moreover, how adaptable ideas are plays a crucial role in their survival. Just like species need to adjust to their changing environments, ideas also need to be flexible and open to feedback. A great example of this adaptability can be seen in how our understanding of justice has changed—from a focus on punishment to a more restorative approach that prioritizes healing and mending relationships. As society's views shift, so too does our interpretation of justice, showing that ideas are not fixed; they can grow and change in response to new insights and demands.

In this light, adaptability becomes key to survival. Ideas that refuse to change risk becoming outdated, irrelevant in a world that is continuously evolving. This is particularly true for social justice movements, which have adapted to include a wider range of perspectives and issues. For instance, the concept of intersectionality has become essential, recognizing that people experience oppression in different ways based on their race, gender, sexuality, and economic status. This deeper understanding has enabled social justice movements to connect with a broader audience, fostering inclusivity and paving the way for more effective solutions.

Technology now plays a dual role as both a supporter and challenger of ideas, adding further complexity to how ideas survive. The rise of social media has dramatically changed how ideas are shared and accepted. On one hand, these online spaces amplify voices that might have been quiet before, helping grassroots movements gain traction and connect people across distances. Movements like #BlackLivesMatter and #MeToo have used technology to spread their messages, mobilizing support and pushing for social change on an unprecedented scale.

However, technology's role is not straightforward. The same platforms that help some ideas gain ground can also hinder others. The quick spread of misinformation and extreme beliefs shows how technology can warp public discussions, leading to divisions and conflict. The balance of influence in these digital spaces often determines which ideas gain support and which are pushed to the sidelines. As we observe the rise and fall of ideas in the online world, it's clear that technology is a double-edged sword; it can elevate vital issues while also endangering the quality of our discussions.

The fate of ideas has broader implications beyond individual concepts. They ripple through society, shaping cultural narratives and influencing how we behave as a group. When some ideas succeed, they can drive progress, spark innovation, and inspire change. Conversely, when certain ideologies fade away, they can hinder growth and limit our ability to tackle pressing societal problems. The disappearance of an idea often creates a vacuum, which can lead to stagnation or the emergence of potentially harmful beliefs. Understanding how ideas survive is critical to grasping how our culture evolves over time.

Reflecting on the historical context of ideas that have slipped into obscurity can be eye-opening. For instance, the decline of colonialist views has opened the door for more balanced discussions about global relations and cultural exchange. The fading of those outdated perspectives is a sign of progress toward a more inclusive understanding of our interconnected world. But what occurs when the prevailing ideas overlook the needs of marginalized communities? This absence can lead to a comeback of harmful ideologies, continuing cycles of oppression and injustice. Thus, the survival of the fittest ideas serves as a mirror, reflecting society's values and priorities and highlighting the complexities of our cultural evolution.

As we navigate this complex landscape, it's beneficial to think about how we can shape the ideas around us. Engaging thoughtfully with the narratives we encounter encourages us to question existing beliefs and advocate for those that resonate with our shared humanity. It prompts us to consider which ideas we choose to support and which we allow to fade away. The survival of ideas isn't just an abstract concept; it's a call to action, inviting us to actively participate in the cultural discussions that shape our lives.

In the end, the survival of the fittest ideas highlights the need to nurture an environment where diverse viewpoints can thrive alongside one another. By encouraging adaptability, relevance, and inclusivity, we can create a rich intellectual ecosystem that promotes innovative thinking and social progress. The ability of ideas to grow, connect with the needs of society, and utilize technology wisely will shape the future we all share.

As we look forward, we must stay aware of how powerful ideas can be in molding our world. The stories we tell, the beliefs we embrace, and the concepts we support have the ability to either uplift or undermine our communities. In this ongoing battle for survival, we need to be careful with the choices we make, working to nurture ideas that not only last but also inspire and empower.

Together, we can help ensure that the ideas shaping our culture promote understanding, inclusivity, and positive change. The survival of the fittest ideas calls for our attention, engagement, and commitment to building a world that reflects our highest hopes for humanity.

Peter Whitmore

Chapter 8: Barriers to Ideological Spread

Cognitive Immunity: Defenses Against New Ideas

When we think about how ideas spread, it's easy to compare the process to how diseases are transmitted. Just like our bodies have immune systems to fight off infections, our minds have their own kind of cognitive immunity that protects us from an overwhelming flood of new ideas. This cognitive immunity isn't just a passive barrier; it consists of complex mental processes that influence how we take in information and interact with the world around us. It's like a system of checks and balances that can shield us from harmful beliefs, but at the same time, it can make it hard for us to accept ideas that might actually help us.

Cognitive biases sit at the core of cognitive immunity—those little quirks in our thinking that can lead us to irrational conclusions and strengthen our current beliefs. These biases act as shortcuts for our minds, making decisions easier but also creating roadblocks to accepting new ideas. For example, confirmation bias is a common cognitive bias that drives people to look for information that supports their existing beliefs, while ignoring or downplaying evidence that challenges them. Picture someone who strongly believes in a certain political view. This person is likely to seek out news sources that back up their opinions, creating a bubble of information that only reinforces what they already think. Consequently, they may become so set in their views that they find it hard to consider other perspectives.

This isn't just a political issue; confirmation bias can happen in many areas—like health, economics, or social matters. It creates echo chambers where differing opinions aren't just brushed aside but actively attacked. This is especially concerning in our social media-driven world, where ideas can spread rapidly. In this context, an individual takes on the role of a gatekeeper, conveniently filtering out anything that might challenge their comfortable beliefs. Even when faced with solid evidence that contradicts their views, their cognitive bias can act as a sort of protective shield, leading them to dismiss it outright.

Another cognitive bias that can seriously block the acceptance of new ideas is called anchoring. This happens when people cling too tightly to the first piece of information they encounter while making decisions. Whether it's a statistic, an opinion, or a fact, that initial information becomes an anchor, and everything else is compared against it. For instance, if someone reads a flashy headline claiming that a new diet guarantees quick weight loss, that person might latch onto the idea of that diet's effectiveness. If they later come across scientific studies that suggest otherwise, they might struggle to accept those findings because they're mentally stuck on the first claim. This shows how our beliefs can become rigid, making it hard to adapt to new information or viewpoints.

The Dunning-Kruger effect is another cognitive bias that contributes to our cognitive immunity. This occurs when individuals with limited knowledge or skill overestimate their own competence. Think about someone who believes they fully understand a complicated scientific topic, even though they lack the necessary expertise. Their overconfidence can lead them to dismiss professional opinions or nuanced arguments. While this self-assuredness might feel protective, it often results in ignoring valuable insights that could help them gain a better understanding of the issue at hand.

While cognitive biases can help shield us from harmful ideas, they can also create significant obstacles when it comes to accepting new, helpful concepts. Healthy skepticism can be a virtue in our search for truth, encouraging us to question claims, seek evidence, and think critically. However, if skepticism goes too far, it can turn into a stubborn resistance to new ideas. This is where it becomes vital to strike a balance between skepticism and openness. We need to learn how to balance our natural doubts with a willingness to explore and entertain fresh perspectives. Developing critical thinking skills can help us navigate the confusing waters of conflicting information, allowing us to differentiate between valid arguments and baseless claims.

Moreover, the stories we tell ourselves and our identities shape how we process ideas. We often hold emotional connections to our personal narratives about who we are and what we believe. Questioning these narratives can feel like a threat to our very existence. Imagine someone who has built their identity around certain beliefs—whether they're religious, political, or social. When faced with information that contradicts those beliefs, it's not just an intellectual challenge; it feels like a direct attack on who they are. This resistance to new ideas isn't just about the ideas themselves; it's deeply tied to our identities.

A striking example of this dynamic can be seen in political polarization. People often align themselves with specific parties or movements, creating identities closely linked to their ideological beliefs. This partisanship can lead to echo chambers where opposing views are minimized, and loyalty to the group takes precedence. In these situations, cognitive immunity is fully engaged, as individuals not only reject conflicting viewpoints but also feel pressured to defend their stance even when faced with evidence that suggests otherwise.

A noteworthy case study highlighting this cognitive immunity is the growing extreme partisanship in today's politics. As political affiliations become more polarized, the mental defenses people use to maintain their beliefs grow stronger. Research conducted by social psychologists found that individuals who strongly identify with a political party were less likely to accept information that went against their party's platform, even if that information came from a source they usually trusted.

Essentially, these individuals chose loyalty to their party over a commitment to the truth. This paints a vivid picture of cognitive immunity in action: the desire to belong to a group and uphold its values can overshadow the quest for genuine understanding.

Understanding the complexities of cognitive immunity requires us to appreciate the psychological mechanisms at play. While it's crucial to protect ourselves from harmful ideologies, it's just as important to remain open to new ideas and perspectives. Finding this balance can empower us to engage in meaningful conversations and create a more inclusive atmosphere for intellectual growth. The journey toward understanding different viewpoints isn't just about absorbing new information; it requires a willingness to confront our biases, challenge our narratives, and embrace the discomfort that can come with personal growth.

In a world filled with diverse ideas and viewpoints, the obstacles to sharing and accepting new ideas often lie not in the ideas themselves, but within our own minds. By recognizing the workings of cognitive immunity, we can start to question our biases and rethink the narratives that define us. This awareness encourages us to engage with the world in a more open and thoughtful way, ultimately creating an environment where new ideas can thrive. The battle against cognitive immunity isn't about getting rid of skepticism or shielding ourselves from all ideas. Instead, it's about learning how to harness our cognitive defenses while staying open to the transformative power that new perspectives can bring. This journey not only enriches our understanding of the world but also sets the stage for greater dialogue, exchange, and, hopefully, collective growth.

Cultural and Social Resistance: The Weight of Existing Beliefs

In every corner of the world, cultural stories and traditions shape how people think, believe, and behave. These stories are not just tales passed down through generations; they are deeply rooted in society and often set the limits on what is considered acceptable thought. When new ideas try to break through this thick layer of cultural history, they frequently face strong resistance. This resistance is not just an abstract idea; it is a powerful force that affects how individuals and groups make decisions. It stirs up emotions and can lead people to become defensive when faced with ideas that challenge their established beliefs.

Consider the rich world of indigenous beliefs, which often emphasize a strong connection to the land and nature. These belief systems, built over thousands of years, carry a sense of identity and continuity that modern scientific ideas sometimes seem to threaten. Indigenous communities worldwide have faced ongoing pressure to conform to dominant cultures that favor industrialization and technological progress. This clash often sparks a cultural backlash, leading to a passionate defense of traditional practices and viewpoints. The lengths people go to in order to protect their cultural identity can be truly inspiring. Many engage in protests, education, and community-building efforts to push back against the encroaching ideologies that threaten their way of life.

Social conditioning also plays a vital role in shaping our beliefs and attitudes. From an early age, we are influenced by the social environments around us. Family, friends, and broader societal norms create a framework within which we develop our beliefs. The pressure to fit in can be overwhelming, often resulting in a conflict between personal convictions and group identity. This is especially noticeable in workplaces, where groupthink can stifle creativity and innovation as people prioritize harmony over expressing dissent. The fear of being left out can push individuals to hide their true opinions in order to go along with the majority.

Picture a situation where an employee shares an innovative idea during a team meeting. If that idea is met with skepticism or outright rejection, the employee might quickly withdraw, feeling not only disappointed but also uncertain about their own judgment. Conversely, if the team enthusiastically supports the idea, the employee may feel empowered, sparking a wave of creativity and innovation. This example highlights the influence of social proof in shaping our beliefs. The desire for acceptance within social groups can motivate people to endorse certain ideologies while discouraging others. Over time, this dynamic can solidify existing beliefs, making new ideas feel unfamiliar and unwelcome.

Collective identity adds another layer of complexity to the spread of ideas. Humans are naturally social beings, and our identities are often tied to the groups we belong to—whether that's based on nationality, religion, or political views. Loyalty to one's group can lead to a rejection of ideas from outside that group. This sense of tribalism can show up in different ways, from casually dismissing differing opinions to engaging in hostile arguments.

Nationalism, for instance, can serve as a strong barrier to accepting new ideas. When people strongly identify with their nation, they may see foreign concepts as threats to their cultural identity. Throughout history, political movements have thrived on this sense of nationalism, often using fear and mistrust of outsiders to gain support. This is evident in populist movements that long for a simpler past, painting new ideas as dangerous forces that could disrupt the social order.

Understanding the historical context helps us grasp the reasons behind ideological resistance. Take the Enlightenment period, when reason and scientific inquiry challenged established religious norms. The thinkers of the Enlightenment met significant backlash for challenging the dominant beliefs of their time. Yet, over the years, the very ideas that faced strong opposition became foundational to modern thinking. This contrast reveals an important truth: while cultural resistance can be strong, it is not impossible to overcome.

When we look at the historical conflict between established ideas and new ones, we can see parallels in today's society. The discussions around climate change, for example, serve as a snapshot of the resistance that new ideas encounter. Despite overwhelming scientific agreement, many cling to outdated beliefs that prioritize immediate economic benefits over long-term environmental health. The social conditioning that links economic growth with success, combined with a collective identity rooted in consumerism, can create a significant barrier to embracing new environmental ideas.

Education plays a crucial role in this scenario. While education is often seen as a powerful tool for spreading new ideas, it can also reinforce existing beliefs. When individuals learn in systems that emphasize certain narratives while ignoring others, they develop a distorted view of the world. This can lead to a form of intellectual elitism, where those with access to specific knowledge dismiss alternative viewpoints as uninformed or backward. This divide creates a gap between those with particular knowledge and those without, further deepening societal divisions.

Engaging with new ideas takes more than just exposure; it requires a readiness to critically examine and question our deeply held beliefs. The interplay of cultural and social influences creates a fertile ground for resistance, as people navigate the complexities of their identities, communities, and traditions. By recognizing the burdens of existing beliefs, we can better understand the challenges we face in fostering acceptance of new ideas.

The stories we tell ourselves about who we are and what we believe hold great power. They shape how we see the world and influence our realities. When confronted with new ideas that challenge these narratives, individuals often react strongly. This is clear in discussions about contentious issues like climate change, immigration, or social justice. For many, these topics are not just abstract ideas; they are closely connected to their sense of self and belonging.

Imagine someone who has built their identity around a specific political belief. When faced with information that contradicts their views, it isn't just an academic disagreement; it feels like a personal threat. The instinctive response is often to dig in and defend those beliefs fiercely, rather than considering the possibility of change. This psychological reaction highlights the significant obstacles to spreading new ideas.

The emotional weight of established beliefs can show in various ways. For example, think about how people react during heated debates about social issues. They may become defensive and resort to personal attacks instead of having constructive conversations. The fear of being labeled as ignorant or misguided can cause individuals to reject opposing viewpoints reflexively. This tendency is heightened in our hyper-connected world, where social media can create echo chambers, amplifying existing beliefs and drowning out dissent.

As we reflect on the complex web of cultural narratives, social conditioning, and shared identities, it becomes evident that the barriers to spreading new ideas are not just intellectual hurdles; they are deeply emotional and psychological. The weight of existing beliefs can feel overwhelming, creating an environment where new ideas struggle to take root.

Yet, there is a glimmer of hope. History teaches us that cultural and social resistance is not always rigid or unyielding. The evolution of societal beliefs often happens in waves, driven by shifts in collective awareness. Movements for civil rights, gender equality, and environmental sustainability have all challenged outdated norms and ideologies. These movements have sparked conversations, fostered connections, and ultimately led to meaningful change in society.

The path toward embracing new ideas is not a straight line. It comes with setbacks and challenges, but it is also filled with moments of profound transformation. The narratives that define us and our cultures can be rewritten, opening up possibilities for growth and evolution. By engaging with complexity and embracing the discomfort that comes from questioning our beliefs, we can start to navigate the intricate landscape of ideological change.

In this effort, empathy is key. To truly understand the weight of existing beliefs, we must seek to grasp the stories that shape them. Listening to others, even when their beliefs differ from ours, can create space for dialogue and connection. It encourages us to break through the barriers that separate us and engage with the rich variety of ideas present in our world.

As we confront the challenges of spreading new ideas, we need to acknowledge the tremendous power of cultural and social dynamics. These forces can either hinder or help the acceptance of fresh concepts. By embracing the complexity of these dynamics and nurturing an openness to change, we can create a more welcoming environment for discussion and growth. The weight of existing beliefs is significant, but it is not unmovable. With patience, understanding, and a readiness to engage, we can pave the way for transformative shifts in thought that reflect the evolving nature of our shared humanity.

Information Overload: The Drowning of Competing Messages

In today's busy world, our online environment feels like a chaotic marketplace where information is constantly shouting for our attention. The amount of messages, opinions, and data that bombards us every day can be truly astonishing. Each time our phone pings, we scroll through screens, or refresh news updates, we add to a swirling mix of noise that can lead to something many of us know all too well: information overload. This is a reality that many of us experience, yet few truly understand. To grasp how this flood of information affects our beliefs and viewpoints, we need to explore what information overload really means.

At its heart, information overload happens when there's just too much information available, making it hard for us to process or understand it. It's like being hit by a wave of data that overwhelms our brains, causing us to shut down under the strain. This mental overload can have serious effects on our minds. Studies show that when we're drowning in information, our ability to make decisions gets muddled. Instead of gaining a clearer view of the world, the flood of ideas often leaves us confused, indecisive, and clinging to what we already know. This is where the paradox of choice comes in: when we're faced with too many options, we often freeze up, unable to choose anything at all.

The effects of this overload go beyond just being annoying. It can twist how we form our beliefs, leading us to grab onto ideas that fit neatly with what we already think, instead of exploring new viewpoints. Our brains are naturally wired to find patterns and make sense of our surroundings. But when we're hit with a wave of conflicting information, it becomes tough to tell what's true and what's just noise. This is especially worrying in a time when misinformation and disinformation spread like wildfire on social media, often posing as trustworthy content. Because of this, people can find themselves stuck in echo chambers where their current beliefs get reinforced rather than challenged, widening the gaps between different perspectives.

When we look at the impact of competing messages in this overloaded information world, the situation gets even trickier. The internet, once celebrated as a great equalizer of information, has turned into a battleground where different stories fight for our attention. With everyone vying for our focus, powerful ideas often get lost in the chaos, diluted or completely drowned out. Think back to the last time you scrolled through your social media feed—was it a simple experience? Chances are, it was a whirlwind of posts, videos, and articles all clamoring for a piece of your attention. Each piece of content is like a competitor in a race, and often, in that struggle, the true message gets overlooked.

Now, let's think about how this competition plays out in politics. During elections, for example, candidates and parties fill media channels with messages designed to sway us. At the same time, grassroots movements, fact-checkers, and opposing narratives pop up, each trying to promote their version of the truth. The outcome? A landscape so fragmented that it's tough for people to tell reliable information from exaggerated claims. This dilution of powerful ideas means even the most well-researched viewpoints struggle to catch on.

This confusion doesn't just complicate things; it also breeds skepticism. As people sift through so many competing messages, they might become cynical, questioning the motives behind everything they read. This skepticism can eventually lead to apathy, making them less interested in engaging with new ideas at all. When every piece of information feels questionable, the tendency to dismiss rather than explore can take over. In this climate, finding meaning becomes a real challenge. How can anyone build solid beliefs when the very foundation of the information they rely on feels shaky?

It's here that the heavy burden of information overload becomes clear. The constant influx of new ideas creates a space filled with uncertainty, where forming clear beliefs becomes difficult. The more messages that clash with their existing views, the less likely people are to explore unfamiliar concepts. The mental discomfort that arises when new information clashes with what we already believe can lead to frustration and exhaustion, pushing us back toward the comfort of our familiar ideologies. Instead of encouraging curiosity and open-mindedness, this information-heavy environment can, ironically, wear us out.

We can see the strong effects of information overload on belief formation in the rise of conspiracy theories in recent years. In a world overflowing with information, the appeal of alternative explanations and unfounded beliefs has gained traction, often flourishing in a setting that should promote knowledge. Conspiracy theories thrive on the chaos of information overload, frequently presenting themselves as the "hidden truth" within the noise. They offer simpler stories that seem to make sense in a world that feels increasingly complicated. In this way, the flood of information can lead to the rise of baseless beliefs, making the already tricky landscape of belief acceptance even harder.

Take the spread of conspiracy theories around events like the COVID-19 pandemic, for example. In the early days of the outbreak, people faced a storm of information—scientific studies, government announcements, personal stories. Amid this confusion, questionable claims and conspiracy theories popped up, taking advantage of the uncertainty that so many were feeling. Those looking for clarity often found themselves drawn to these simpler but misleading narratives, which provided a sense of understanding in turbulent times. The constant challenge to what was seen as credible information left many feeling lost and doubtful of trustworthy sources.

This scenario serves as a powerful reminder of how information overload can twist our view of reality, leading to a space where unfounded beliefs can thrive. The relentless competition for our attention among various stories can push individuals toward viewpoints that might lack solid evidence but resonate with their emotional needs. The mental challenges at play—cognitive overload, skepticism, and disinterest—create an environment where misinformation can easily take root.

Navigating this tricky web of competing messages requires a skill that many find tough to master. As we try to cut through the noise, knowing how to critically evaluate information becomes crucial. This means not only checking the credibility of sources but also recognizing the biases that might shape how we interpret what we read. It's a skill that takes time and effort to develop, but it's more important than ever in a world filled with information overload.

To counter the risks of information overload, we need to build an environment that encourages thoughtful discussions. Creating spaces for open conversations that focus on active listening can help bring in a variety of viewpoints. People shouldn't just be exposed to new ideas; they should engage with them meaningfully. By promoting a culture of curiosity instead of defensiveness, we can start to bridge the divides that information overload has created.

In the end, the challenge of information overload isn't just a personal battle; it reflects wider societal issues. The need for clarity amidst the chaos has never been more urgent. As we navigate the complexities of forming beliefs and accepting different viewpoints, we must recognize the influences at work and work to create spaces that promote understanding, empathy, and open-mindedness. By doing this, we can start to unravel the confusion and apathy that define the current ideological landscape, paving the way for meaningful conversations and transformative ideas.

The digital age has opened the door to incredible opportunities for sharing thoughts, but it has also brought in a wave of overwhelming noise. As we face this reality, it's vital to prioritize discernment, empathy, and critical thinking. By understanding the dangers of information overload and how it affects our beliefs, we can take significant steps toward building a more informed, open, and ideologically diverse society.

Chapter 9: Harnessing Virality

Strategies for Spreading Ideas

In our connected world, where a single tweet can ripple across the globe in seconds, spreading ideas is a valuable skill and a powerful tool. Picture yourself standing in a bustling street, trying to shout your message to the crowd. Instead of a few curious faces turning your way, imagine your words reaching thousands, maybe even millions, through the vast internet. That's the magic of going viral—creating a message so engaging that it doesn't just grab attention; it motivates people to take action.

The first step on this exciting journey is to understand who you're trying to reach and what makes them tick. To develop ideas that really resonate, take a moment to see things from your audience's perspective. This means doing some research and paying close attention to what people say, share, and like. You need to tap into their hopes, fears, and dreams. A great example of this is the Ice Bucket Challenge, which swept social media in 2014. At first, the idea of dumping ice water over your head might seem silly. But what made it take off was its emotional core: it was fun, it was a challenge, and it supported a serious cause—the fight against ALS. This campaign didn't just ask for donations; it invited everyone to join in a shared experience that deeply resonated with their values.

Next, storytelling becomes a key player in the quest for virality. Stories connect us by drawing from our common human experiences. They make ideas relatable and unforgettable. When you tell a story, you're not just sharing facts; you're creating a vivid scene that stirs emotions. A classic example is the "Dove Real Beauty Sketches" campaign. In this powerful narrative, women were sketched by a forensic artist, who could only capture their true beauty through how they viewed themselves. This campaign sparked an important conversation about self-esteem and body image. It wasn't merely a marketing tactic; it was a heartfelt story that resonated with audiences, encouraging them to share it widely.

When you're crafting your message, think about how it connects emotionally. Emotions drive people to act, and in the digital world, they are what spark shares and likes. Positive feelings, like joy or surprise, can lead to more shares, while negative emotions, such as anger or sadness, can engage people differently.

Research shows that content that triggers strong emotional reactions is more likely to be shared. This is the driving force behind successful viral campaigns like "#MeToo," which was built on personal stories of strength and empowerment. It ignited a global conversation about sexual assault and harassment, allowing individuals to feel seen and heard, inspiring further sharing and solidarity.

Now that we've covered some foundational principles, let's dive into a step-by-step guide for creating content that stands out. Start with a hook that draws people in. This could be a thought-provoking question, a surprising statistic, or even a funny story. The goal is to pique your audience's curiosity and make them want to learn more. For example, a headline like "What If Everything You Knew About Success Was Wrong?" immediately invites readers to explore a new viewpoint.

Once you've captured their interest, keep building on that by providing real value. This could be helpful information, thought-provoking insights, or entertaining stories. Make sure to infuse your message with authenticity; people naturally gravitate toward genuine voices. Take the "Humans of New

York" project, for example. By sharing the diverse stories of everyday people, creator Brandon Stanton not only highlighted the beauty of humanity but also created a sense of community. Each photograph, paired with snippets of a person's life, draws viewers in, forging a deep emotional connection that goes beyond the digital screen.

Another important factor is understanding how each social platform works. Every platform has its own vibe and expectations, so it's crucial to tailor your content to fit in. For instance, Instagram thrives on visuals. A stunning photo that captures an emotion or moment will likely do better than a long text post. On the other hand, Twitter favors concise, impactful statements that can spark discussions and threads.

Working with influencers can also significantly boost the reach of your message. These individuals have built trust with their followers, and when they share your content, it carries weight. A great example is the collaboration between fitness influencer Kayla Itsines and a health food brand. When Kayla posted a recipe featuring the brand's product, her followers not only trusted her recommendation but also felt inspired to recreate and share their experiences, broadening the message's reach.

Make sure your message is easy to share. This could mean including clear calls to action or creating eye-catching graphics and quotes. The "You vs. the World" meme format became a viral hit not just because it was relatable, but also because it was easily adaptable. People could personalize it by adding their own experiences, which encouraged even more sharing.

Lastly, think about the ethical side of spreading ideas. As influential creators or marketers, we need to be aware of the responsibilities that come with our power. It's crucial to ensure that the ideas we promote are based on truth, respect, and empathy. The internet is filled with misinformation, and spreading false narratives can lead to serious consequences. For example, the spread of incorrect health information during the COVID-19 pandemic resulted in harmful behaviors and a loss of trust in reliable sources. So, while the mechanics of going viral make it easy for ideas to spread quickly, ensuring the integrity of your message is vital.

The digital landscape offers both opportunities and challenges. By honing your ability to create messages that reflect audience psychology, leverage storytelling, tap into emotions, and adapt to different platforms, you can effectively harness the power of virality. Plus, being mindful of the ethical implications ensures that your influence is used responsibly.

As you set out to share your ideas, keep in mind: every message has the potential to spark conversations, inspire movements, and create real change. The question isn't just whether your ideas will go viral, but how you'll handle the responsibility that comes with that power. By embracing these strategies, you're not just capturing attention; you're fostering meaningful connections in a world that craves authentic dialogue.

Ethical Considerations

Our minds are like fires, eager to be sparked. A simple idea can light up the darkest corners of our thoughts and the world around us. But with this ability to inspire and influence also comes a big responsibility. We need to make sure the flames we ignite don't get out of control. In today's digital world, where countless voices come together to share, learn, and sometimes twist ideas, we must think seriously about the ethical choices behind the messages we spread. With this power comes not just responsibility, but a deep obligation to use it wisely.

When we share ideas, we should remember that not all messages are created equal. In an environment where false information can spread like wildfire—often faster than the truth—the stakes are higher than ever. The thrill of going viral can be tempting, but it raises important questions we need to consider. What are the effects of our words? How do they impact others? Are we sharing content that encourages understanding and connection, or are we fueling stories that create division and distrust?

The outcomes of what we share can be far-reaching. In a time when opinions can be incredibly polarized, where echo chambers amplify our own beliefs while shutting out different viewpoints, we need to reflect on whether we're helping to bridge gaps or push people further apart. A powerful message can lift us up and bring us together, but it can also reinforce harmful stereotypes or stir up anger. The lines between what is true and what is false are becoming more difficult to see, especially on social media, where likes, shares, and retweets often take priority over honest journalism and accurate reporting.

Consider how misinformation affected crucial election periods. False claims about candidates, made-up stories about voter fraud, and intentional attempts to mislead the public have been used to manipulate opinions. The result? A society filled with skepticism, where trust in institutions erodes and community engagement suffers. The 2016 U.S. presidential election is a perfect example of how twisted truths can have real impacts, with misinformation spreading rapidly and leading to anxiety, confusion, and growing distrust of the media. This manipulation of information isn't just a political problem; it's an ethical issue that calls for reflection from everyone who shares their thoughts and ideas.

If we look back at the history of viral campaigns, we can see that ethical implications can swing dramatically. On one hand, there are campaigns like the "Ice Bucket Challenge," which raised awareness and funds for ALS research. In this instance, authenticity, transparency, and community spirit came together, showing the power of collective action for good. On the flip side, there are campaigns that spread harmful stereotypes or false narratives, causing social unrest and suffering. The rise of "fake news" highlights just how easily misinformation can thrive without accountability.

As we analyze these examples, it's clear that we need ethical guidelines to help navigate the tricky waters of sharing information. These guidelines shouldn't be seen as restrictions; instead, they should serve as tools that lead us toward responsible communication. They should remind us to think about what our words mean and how they can affect people beyond our immediate circles. An ethical storyteller understands that every story can shape perceptions, influence decisions, and impact lives—whether for better or worse.

To navigate this complex landscape, we need to hold ourselves accountable. Every time we share an idea, we're contributing to a larger conversation—one that can either uplift or tear down. The responsibility doesn't just lie with those who create content but also with those who consume it. As information consumers, we should develop a critical mindset, questioning the sources and intentions behind the stories we come across. It's not enough to simply accept information; we must actively engage with it, distinguishing truth from falsehood while checking our own biases along the way.

When we craft messages, ethical storytelling should always be our main focus. Honesty and integrity should be the foundation of our narratives. Authenticity can cut through the clutter surrounding us, building trust and connection with our audiences. When people feel that a creator is genuine—grounded in truth and empathy—they're more likely to engage thoughtfully, share responsibly, and help create a culture of openness. The "Humans of New York" project is a beautiful example of this. By sharing the real and often vulnerable stories of everyday people, the project not only shines a light on individual experiences but also fosters community and empathy among its audience.

Beyond promoting accountability and authenticity, we also have to consider the moral implications of our actions. What might seem harmless or funny at first can have unexpected consequences. With the rise of memes, viral challenges, and social media trends, we need to think about the stories we're helping to tell. Are we merely chasing likes and shares, or are we being thoughtful about our contributions?

Take, for example, the "#MeToo" movement. While it became a powerful voice for survivors of sexual assault, it also brought to light the power dynamics in our society. This movement began with individuals bravely sharing their personal stories, exposing the widespread nature of abuse and harassment. It was a moment of awakening, encouraging people to stand up against injustice. But as the message gained traction, it also faced backlash and misinterpretation. Some critics tried to frame it as an attack on men as a whole. This highlights the importance of handling sensitive topics with care, ensuring that the messaging stays focused on raising awareness, encouraging conversations, and seeking justice.

Additionally, in the digital age, we must stay alert to distinguish between genuine commentary and harmful rhetoric. As creators and influencers, we should be cautious about allowing our platforms to spread hate speech or misinformation. Our responsibility includes challenging narratives that maintain systemic inequalities or promote harmful ideas. It's essential for us to use our voices and platforms to advocate for inclusiveness and understanding instead of fostering division and hostility.

The need for ethical considerations in the sharing of ideas is urgent. As we find ourselves in a new era—where the lines between truth and fiction often blur and the effects of our actions carry significant weight—we need to embrace the role of responsible communicators. This means continuously learning about the ethical implications of our messages and their potential impact.

By striving to be ethical storytellers, we have the chance to create a ripple effect of positive change. Each message shared with integrity, each narrative crafted with care, adds to a culture of accountability and authenticity. As we exchange ideas, let's encourage discussions that uplift, educate, and inspire rather than divide or polarize. Every tweet, post, and campaign is a chance to shape narratives that truly matter.

As we navigate the challenges of the digital age, let's embrace a mindset rooted in empathy and responsibility. Recognizing that our words can shape opinions, influence actions, and affect lives, we should approach our responsibilities with humility and integrity. The potential of our ideas to create genuine change is enormous, but harnessing that power ethically calls for a commitment to truth, empathy, and accountability.

In the end, sharing ideas is about more than just what we say; it's also about the principles that guide us. By embracing ethical storytelling, we build a foundation for trust and connection in a digital landscape that can often feel chaotic. The key isn't just how we amplify our voices, but how we do so with mindfulness and care. Let's strive to ignite flames of understanding, compassion, and collaboration—coming together to turn our collective voices into a powerful force for good.

Tools and Metrics

The world of ideas is as colorful and unpredictable as a carnival ride, full of twists and turns that keep us on our toes. But unlike the thrill of a quick ride, sharing ideas takes more than just excitement; it requires careful planning, strategy, and a good grasp of the tools that can help our ideas soar to new heights. So, what sets apart a passing post from a full-blown movement? Often, the answer lies in the tools and metrics we use to gauge how our ideas are landing.

To tap into the power of virality, we first need to get comfortable with various analytics platforms that act as our guideposts in this creative adventure. Tools like Google Analytics, Facebook Insights, and Instagram Analytics unlock important information about how our content performs across different platforms. They give us a peek into our audience's behavior, helping us see what captures their interest and what doesn't quite hit the mark.

Picture logging into Google Analytics and witnessing not just numbers, but a story unfolding. You see visitors coming in from all over the world, each clicking through your well-crafted pages, with every page view showing that your message is making an impact. Metrics like unique visitors, average session duration, and bounce rates come together to tell us about audience engagement. These numbers aren't just statistics; they are the heart and soul of our campaigns, shining a light on what works and what needs a little tweaking.

Next up is Facebook Insights, where you can really feel your audience's heartbeat. Here, you can track how far your posts reach, how many people engage with them, and even learn a bit about who is interacting with your content. Are they young adults living in bustling cities? Parents juggling family life? Or maybe they're a mix of people brought together by shared interests? Understanding these details allows you to better customize your messages, changing them like a chameleon to connect more deeply with what your audience wants.

On the flip side, Instagram Analytics adds a visual flair to how we measure engagement. With its focus on images and stories, Instagram is perfect for telling captivating tales that resonate on a personal level. By diving into likes, shares, comments, and saves, we can see not just what's popular but how genuine our connection with followers is. The heart emojis and encouraging comments offer immediate feedback, showing us those moments when our content clicks and sparks conversations.

However, metrics alone don't paint the whole picture. They need a context, and this is where our creativity and instincts come in. While numbers can show us trends and areas for improvement, they often miss the emotional layers of our messages. Yes, making decisions based on data is crucial, but it's just as important to blend those insights with our understanding of people's feelings and motivations. Behind every click and share is a real person with their own thoughts and emotions.

To amplify our messaging and boost its chances of going viral, consider using A/B testing. This strategy involves trying out different versions of content to see what resonates best with your audience. Imagine you have two headlines for the same article: one that piques curiosity and another that promises valuable insights. By showing each version to different groups, you can find out which one grabs more attention. This trial-and-error approach isn't just a fun exercise; it's a strategic way to refine our messaging as we go.

A/B testing encourages us to push boundaries and venture into new territory. It's like being a playful scientist in a digital lab, mixing wording, images, and calls to action to discover the ultimate formula for virality. Maybe one version gets more likes, while another sparks a flurry of shares, and yet another prompts heartfelt comments. No matter the outcome, each test adds to our understanding, helping us zero in on what truly resonates with our audience.

Don't forget the importance of audience segmentation, too. This practice is all about breaking your audience into different groups based on shared traits like age, location, interests, and behaviors. By crafting messages for each segment, you create a more tailored experience that speaks directly to your audience's hearts and minds. When communication feels personal, it makes it much more likely that your ideas will spread like wildfire.

Think of audience segmentation like an artist choosing colors for a painting. Each shade—every demographic and psychographic insight—adds depth and vibrancy to the work. When you consider the various layers of your audience and create messages that reflect their specific experiences and preferences, you turn a simple campaign into a rich, multi-dimensional experience that captivates and inspires.

Of course, keeping an eye on new technologies and trends is just as vital as understanding today's metrics. The digital communication landscape is always changing, shaped by advancements in artificial intelligence and machine learning. These innovations are more than just buzzwords; they are powerful tools that can enhance how our ideas spread and help us refine our strategies based on solid data.

AI can analyze massive amounts of data at lightning speed, spotting hidden patterns in audience behavior and preferences. Imagine the power of machine learning algorithms predicting which types of content will resonate with different audience segments, allowing you to craft messages that are not only timely but also relevant. By harnessing these technologies, you put yourself at the forefront of spreading ideas, ready to adapt and evolve in an ever-changing digital world.

Yet, technology shouldn't steal the spotlight from the human touch in our messaging. While algorithms can guide us, it's our creativity, empathy, and instincts that bring those insights to life. The best ideas come from a genuine place of connection, where data and personal experience blend seamlessly. Finding this balance is key to building a culture of innovation and virality that stands the test of time.

As you navigate this complex landscape of tools and metrics, remember that your goal isn't just to gather data but to interpret it meaningfully. Take a moment to reflect on what the numbers are saying and how they align with your mission. Are you creating content that informs, inspires, and empowers? Are you building connections that go beyond the screen?

In this ongoing journey of measurement and evaluation, let curiosity be your guide. Challenge yourself to dig deeper:

What really engages your audience? What keeps them interested, and what makes them want to share? The answers might be hidden in the subtleties of your language, the emotional power of your visuals, or the authenticity of your stories. Each interaction is a learning moment, a chance to tweak your approach and ensure your ideas not only gain traction but also leave a lasting impression.

Ultimately, the tools and metrics we have are powerful partners in our quest for virality. They offer clarity and direction, helping us craft messages that resonate in a busy digital landscape. By embracing a data-driven mindset while staying grounded in creativity and empathy, we can turn our ideas into movements that inspire change, foster community, and create a wave of positive engagement.

So as you move forward with insights, reflections, and a toolkit of valuable resources, keep the spirit of experimentation alive. Be bold in your approach, ready to test new ideas and strategies. In this dance between creativity and analytics, remember that every click, share, and comment brings you closer to understanding how to amplify your voice and ensure your ideas reach far and wide. The journey may be intricate, but the potential for impact is boundless, waiting for you to grasp it with authenticity, insight, and purpose.

Chapter 10: Navigating a World of Viral Ideas

Becoming an Informed Participant

In a world bursting with information, it can feel like trying to swim upstream in a raging river. Navigating through all these ideas isn't just a helpful skill—it's a vital part of staying afloat. Think of becoming an informed participant as learning to sail expertly through these waters. You'll need a compass and a map to steer clear of the rocky shores of misinformation and bias. The first step on this journey is finding credible information. While this might sound simple, it requires effort and a sharp eye for detail.

Picture yourself stepping into a library, where the whispers of knowledge fill the air. The shelves are packed with books, each one eager to share its story, argument, or perspective. The real challenge is figuring out which stories are based on facts and which are just shadows of the truth. Your first tool in this quest should be the ability to check the credentials of the authors you encounter. This means looking closely and asking questions like, "What makes this author an expert?" or "What experiences shape their views?"

Understanding an author's background can make a big difference. For example, a historian might have a more informed perspective on today's social issues than someone from a marketing background simply because of their training and experience.

But credentials alone don't paint the full picture. It's also vital to confirm facts by checking multiple sources. The internet can sometimes feel like a bustling bazaar filled with all kinds of information—some of it solid and reliable, while much of it is more like a circus of half-truths and outright lies. Trusted websites dedicated to fact-checking and respected news organizations can act as your reliable guides through this chaotic landscape. When you come across a claim that seems too outrageous or convenient, take a moment to hit the brakes and look for other viewpoints. Like a detective piecing together clues, you should gather verified information from different angles to figure out the truth of an idea.

Logical fallacies can sneak into arguments, disguising themselves as solid reasoning and tempting you to believe in their certainty. Learning about common fallacies, such as the straw man or ad hominem attacks, can help you notice when an argument isn't as rational as it seems. A strong argument stands firm like a sturdy fortress, while a fallacious one is more like a house of cards, teetering on the edge of collapse. The skill of spotting these reasoning traps sharpens your critical thinking and prepares you to engage thoughtfully with the ideas you encounter.

Beyond just evaluating information, it's important to consider the context in which ideas are born. Ideas don't float in a vacuum; they're shaped by the history, society, and culture around them. Take viral memes, for instance. These digital snippets often carry deeper meanings that can change dramatically depending on the situation. A meme that makes fun of a political figure might make some people laugh while making others upset, all based on the social attitudes at the time. To truly understand an idea, you need to peel back the layers and look at the circumstances that created it.

Think about the social movements that arise from issues of injustice. The ideas fueling these movements are often intertwined with a complex history of grievances, cultural stories, and shared memories. Understanding this background helps you appreciate the subtleties of the ideas being pushed forward, allowing for a more meaningful engagement rather than just a surface-level reaction. Grasping the context isn't just important for understanding the present; it can also help you predict the potential future impacts of these ideas based on what has happened before.

Psychological factors also play a big role in how we assess ideas. Everyone sees the world through a personal lens shaped by their own experiences, beliefs, and biases. Cognitive biases can cloud our judgment, often leading us to accept information that confirms what we already think—a tendency known as confirmation bias. This natural inclination can create echo chambers, where we only surround ourselves with ideas that reinforce our views while dismissing opposing thoughts. Being aware of this tendency is a key step toward breaking free from it.

Another common pitfall is the bandwagon effect, where the popularity of an idea can lead us to accept it without questioning it. Just because something is trending doesn't mean it's true or valuable. Remember, trends can be deceiving; just because an idea is popular doesn't mean it's credible. By recognizing these psychological influences, you can develop a more balanced approach to evaluating ideas, pushing yourself to step outside your comfort zone and challenge your own beliefs.

Becoming an informed participant isn't just about evaluating ideas; it's also about nurturing a mindset of curiosity and open-mindedness. Embrace the idea that it's perfectly fine to ask questions, seek out different viewpoints, and engage in meaningful conversations. This openness can deepen your understanding of various issues and bring new insights that might otherwise have stayed hidden.

As you hone your critical thinking skills, you transform from a passive consumer of ideas into an active contributor to the conversation. You're no longer just absorbing information; you're ready to challenge assumptions and stand up for well-supported viewpoints. Your voice becomes part of a rich dialogue, enhancing the discussion around important topics.

In this constantly shifting landscape of ideas, where new thoughts can spread like wildfire, being able to critically assess the information around you is more than just helpful; it's a necessary skill. With the right tools and a mindset geared toward inquiry, you can navigate the complexities of modern ideologies, making informed choices that enrich your understanding and empower others as well.

Equipped with this toolkit, you're ready to engage thoughtfully with the flood of ideas that surrounds us. The journey of becoming an informed participant is ongoing, filled with moments of reflection, debate, and personal growth. Each new idea you encounter is an opportunity to broaden your perspective and contribute meaningfully to the discussions shaping our world, helping to build a more thoughtful and informed society.

Influencing Positively

Ideas are like seeds drifting in the wind, looking for a place to land and grow. In our hyper-connected world, both good and bad ideas can spread quickly, shaping how we think and act. While we've talked about the importance of being informed and thinking critically, it's just as crucial to think about how we can share ideas that encourage growth and understanding. When we speak with purpose and care, we can lift up the positive ideas that create meaningful change, pushing back against harmful beliefs that can take hold.

Let's kick off this discussion by looking at the power of communication—specifically, the key ideas of empathy, active listening, and clarity. Communication isn't just about passing along information; it's how we connect with one another as human beings. In a world that often feels divided, being able to engage with empathy can truly make a difference. Empathy helps us recognize the experiences and viewpoints of others, creating a space where open conversations can happen. It reminds us that every idea comes from a person—someone who has hopes, fears, dreams, and stories to share.

Imagine a community meeting where differing opinions come together. Instead of shouting and arguing, everyone takes a moment to listen. They try to understand not only the words being said but also the feelings and backgrounds that shape those words. "Can you tell me why you feel that way?" one person might ask, creating an opening for a meaningful conversation. This simple question can change the mood of a discussion, shifting it from conflict to cooperation. By practicing active listening, we foster a culture of respect, allowing new ideas to emerge and be examined together.

Clarity in how we communicate is just as important. It's not enough to have good intentions; we need to express our ideas in a way that connects with others. This involves thinking carefully about our audience and the context of our messages. A well-formed statement can cut through the noise, letting our ideas shine. We can achieve this by organizing our thoughts, using clear language, and sharing relatable examples. Good communicators often break down complicated ideas into simple, understandable pieces, helping their listeners grasp the heart of their message. When we communicate clearly, we not only improve understanding but also build trust—an essential ingredient in positively influencing others.

Now, let's shift our focus to storytelling, a powerful way to share and advocate for positive ideas. People are naturally drawn to stories. Our brains are wired to respond to narratives, which often connect with us more deeply than dry facts or statistics. For instance, instead of just sharing numbers about climate change, someone might tell their personal story about seeing the impacts of rising sea levels on their coastal town. This personal touch builds empathy and understanding, making complex issues feel real and urgent.

When using storytelling to spread ideas, it's vital to choose stories that are inclusive and represent a variety of experiences. By including different perspectives, we create a richer understanding of the issues we discuss. This inclusivity not only makes our messages more relatable but also respects the diverse experiences that shape our viewpoints. After all, a good story doesn't just engage; it invites others to see themselves within it.

To highlight the impact of grassroots movements in pushing for positive change, let's look at some notable examples where collective action has made a difference. One standout case is the powerful rise of the Black Lives Matter movement. Emerging in response to systemic racism and police violence, this movement has educated millions and sparked important conversations about racial inequality. Activists have harnessed social media to share personal stories, organize protests, and rally support, creating a wave of awareness and dialogue. The emotional weight of their stories has struck a chord, inspiring people from all backgrounds to join the fight for justice and equality.

Another inspiring example is the global environmental movement, which has tapped into grassroots enthusiasm to advocate for climate action. Groups like Fridays for Future, started by young activist Greta Thunberg, have ignited a worldwide awareness of the climate crisis. Through eye-catching campaigns, relatable narratives, and urgent calls to action, these movements have reached millions—especially young people—instilling a sense of urgency and shared responsibility. Social media has been key in amplifying their voices, helping to form strong coalitions across different countries in the battle against climate change.

While these movements have achieved remarkable successes, they've also faced challenges along the way. Learning from their experiences can teach us valuable lessons about advocacy. For example, the difficulties of message saturation and misrepresentation underline the need for careful communication strategies. In an age where information overload is common, a single error can lead to misunderstandings or backlash. Therefore, it's crucial to stay alert, adjusting our messages as needed and keeping communication channels clear.

Ethics play a big role in our advocacy efforts. As we share stories and engage in conversations, we must continually think about the impact of our influence. What are the consequences of the ideas we promote? Are we unintentionally reinforcing harmful stereotypes or leaving out marginalized voices? Being an advocate means committing to inclusivity and respect—traits that should shine through in every interaction.

Inclusivity means more than just using the right words; it's about creating environments where diverse viewpoints are not only welcomed but actively sought. This takes humility and a readiness to listen to people whose experiences differ from our own. It involves understanding that our perspectives are just pieces of a larger puzzle. By putting inclusivity first, we encourage an atmosphere where everyone's voice adds to the conversation, deepening our understanding and boosting our advocacy efforts.

In today's landscape, social media is a powerful tool that can't be ignored. Platforms like Twitter, Instagram, and TikTok have completely changed the way advocacy works. They allow ideas to spread rapidly, reaching huge audiences in moments. However, with this power comes a great deal of responsibility. The risk of miscommunication and the spread of false information is always there. As advocates, we need to be careful about what we share. Every post or share reflects our values and should be approached thoughtfully.

A mindful approach to social media advocacy involves not just creating engaging messages but also having real conversations with our followers. Answering questions, addressing concerns, and encouraging respectful discussions can help build a strong community of supporters. Plus, using strategies like hashtags, teaming up with influencers, and creating content that people want to share can help our messages reach beyond our immediate circles.

While the quickness of social media can be tempting, it's important to balance it with genuine engagement. Real influence doesn't come from likes or shares alone; it comes from building authentic relationships based on trust and shared values. This takes a steady commitment to listening, learning, and adapting our messages to resonate with a variety of audiences.

As we aim to influence positively, it's vital to reflect on our motivations and the impact we wish to achieve. Advocacy should never be about boosting our own egos or seeking validation; instead, it should stem from a sincere desire to create positive change and uplift others. This ethical approach will guide our actions and interactions, ensuring that our influence remains rooted in integrity.

In a world overflowing with ideas, the responsibility to influence positively is not just a privilege but a duty. With the ability to communicate with empathy, listen actively, and share compelling stories, we can become advocates for beneficial ideas. Each of us has the chance to contribute to a richer and more inclusive conversation where diverse thoughts can thrive.

As we move forward on this journey of advocacy, let's keep the power we hold in mind. The ideas we share can inspire, uplift, and connect us all. By creating an atmosphere of thoughtful engagement, empathy, and respect, we can work together to navigate the complex landscape of modern ideas, ensuring that the concepts we support truly uplift humanity and pave the way for a brighter future for everyone. The seeds we plant today will shape the world of tomorrow, and it's up to us to nurture a garden filled with wisdom, understanding, and compassion.

The Future of Ideological Contagion

Imagine a world where ideas spread like wildfire, lighting up minds and hearts in an instant. This is the world we live in today, where new technologies can amplify our beliefs faster than ever before. From artificial intelligence that tailors our news feeds to virtual reality experiences that let us step into different perspectives, the tools we have can be both helpful allies and challenging adversaries in the quest for ideological influence. How we understand and use these technologies will shape not just our personal beliefs, but also the shared values of our communities.

As we approach this exciting new era, it's important to recognize that technology has both bright and dark sides. On one hand, these innovations can help spread uplifting ideas, supporting movements that push for social justice, environmental care, and the well-being of everyone. The speed at which information travels today is astonishing; groundbreaking concepts that once took years to gain traction can now sweep through digital spaces in just a few moments. However, this same speed can also amplify misleading information, creating echo chambers where only certain viewpoints are heard and valued. It's a tricky balance that requires our attention and thoughtful engagement.

Social media platforms, once seen as great equalizers in sharing ideas, have turned into battlegrounds for competing beliefs. The algorithms behind these platforms often prioritize attention-grabbing content over meaningful dialogue, leading to a rise in divisive topics. So, how can we use these technologies for good? The onus is on us—both consumers and creators—to be mindful of the ideas we choose to share. Just like a gardener tending to their plants, we need to take care of our digital spaces, ensuring that harmful ideas don't overshadow those that inspire growth and understanding.

Taking a moment to reflect on our part in this web of ideas is vital. As we navigate the complexities of sharing information, we should ask ourselves some core questions: How can we make sure the ideas we share contribute to a healthier ideological environment? What role do we play as we consume, create, and share content online? These questions encourage us to think deeply about our actions and motivate us to engage in ways that are ethical and constructive.

Think about the potential of new technologies in shaping conversations around us. Artificial intelligence, for example, is already being used to gauge public sentiment and understand which messages truly resonate. This offers a chance for advocates of positive change to refine their communication approaches, using valuable insights to create messages that connect with a wide range of people. Instead of using AI to mislead or manipulate, we could channel its power to spark thoughtful discussions that connect us and foster understanding. By doing this, we can spread ideas that encourage action, not fear.

Virtual reality (VR) presents another exciting way to look at the future of how ideas spread. By placing people in experiences that showcase the challenges and victories of others, VR can create empathy and understanding like no other form of media can. Imagine a world where someone could walk in the shoes of a refugee, experiencing their journey first-hand, or see the effects of climate change on fragile communities. These powerful stories can change how we see things and motivate us to act, pushing us to engage with ideas that promote kindness and teamwork.

In this light, social media platforms also need to take responsibility for their impact on our conversations. They have a huge influence on the ideas that flow through society, and they must commit to transparency and ethical practices. This means designing algorithms that embrace diverse viewpoints, not just those that reinforce existing biases. Picture a social media environment where these algorithms prioritize thoughtful discussions over divisive topics, where people are encouraged to explore ideas that challenge their own. Such a change could foster a culture of openness and understanding, tearing down the walls that keep us apart.

Conclusion

As we conclude our exploration of ideological contagion, it's clear that ideas wield immense power in shaping our world. We've examined how psychological factors, social dynamics, and technological advancements contribute to the viral spread of ideologies.

Remember the case studies we explored – from grassroots movements to internet memes that shifted public discourse. These examples highlight the real-world impact of viral ideas and underscore the importance of understanding this phenomenon.

Armed with the insights from this book, you're now better equipped to navigate the complex landscape of ideas. As you encounter new concepts, remember to approach them critically, considering their origins, spread, and potential consequences.

In this age of rapid information exchange, each of us plays a role in the spread of ideas. By engaging thoughtfully with the ideologies we encounter, we can contribute to more informed and constructive discourse.

The journey doesn't end here. Continue to explore, question, and engage with the ideas shaping our world. Your understanding of ideological contagion is a powerful tool for personal growth and societal progress.

Also by Peter Whitmore:

Mimetic Desire: The Hidden Driver of Culture and Conflict